T0413915

"The sense of place is very highly developed in Southerners."

Flannery O'Connor, 1963

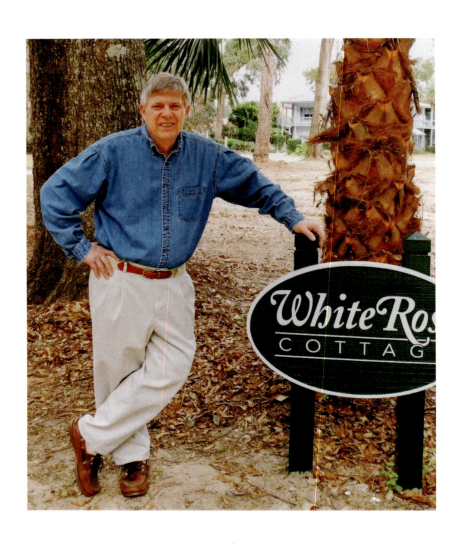

Child-Life on the Tidewater

A Memoir of Coastal Georgia

BUDDY SULLIVAN

2024

*These stories are dedicated
to the memory of the first three generations of the
Sullivan, Hunter and Johnson families that had
a presence in McIntosh County for more than a century,
including my parents, grandparents, and great-grandparents*

A typical low country vista in McIntosh County—marshes, upland, blue sky.

ISBN: 979-8-35093-093-1
Text set in 11-point Goudy Oldstyle. Book design by Buddy Sullivan
All photos by the author unless otherwise indicated
Page 1: Old dock pilings at Shellbluff Creek, Valona
Frontispiece image by Aimee G. Gaddis
Title page: Creighton Island northeast point, and winter marsh

Contents

My great-grandfather Johnson's date palm beside the home I built almost one hundred years later on the site of his original Cedar Point house. As a child I remember this palm as being about half the present height.

Preface

Francis Robert Goulding, a Presbyterian clergyman and author who lived from 1810 to 1881, spent his adolescent years growing up on the McIntosh County, Georgia tidewater, just as I would do a century and a half later. In 1870, Goulding composed an interesting memoir of his early life in the local low country, a book that evoked my own early years in swimming the tidal waters and smelling the salt marsh just as he did. The title of his short book was *Sapelo, or Child-Life on the Tidewater*—the "Sapelo" part of the title referring to the little settlement of Baisden's Bluff on a branch of the tidal Sapelo River, and almost literally an oyster shell's throw across the marsh from the spot at Cedar Point where I spent much of my own early life. Therefore, with full credit to the memory of Rev. Goulding, I resurrect the title of his memoir and apply it to mine, due to the similarities of where we were in our childhood, and the things we experienced. I don't think Rev. Goulding would object, because we both recognize and understand, in spirit and fond memory, the same things about the McIntosh County low country. It is perhaps no coincidence that, in my later life as an adult, I read and re-read a truly epic Southern novel of the low country, *The Prince of Tides*, by my coastal contemporary, the late Pat Conroy, who is far more famous than I am, but with whom I shared an extraordinarily similar upbringing on the coast amid the same ecosystem, the same Southern coastal cultural values and understanding, and similarly embraced by the innocence of the 1950s and 1960s.

The present book originated in 2021 with the publication of the first edition of *Child-Life* as a much lengthier work since it included a sampling of writings from my previously published books about county history. This new edition is more immediate and far more personal since it includes an expanded *Child-Life* memoir, with the addition of memories of my experiences on the local waterways. The book is largely intended for the pleasure and edification of my children, grandchildren, other family members, and friends far and wide. But even the casual reader may find some useful references and be able to relate to my life and associations with the tidewater in similar ways to their own in earlier generations of upbringing.

Buddy Sullivan
White Rose Cottage, January 2024

The marshes of Cedar Point behind my home, looking west toward Baisden's Bluff. The sunsets are always spectacular from here, even in overcast skies. Image by the author used as the cover of *Low Country Historian* (2023)

LOW COUNTRY LEGACY

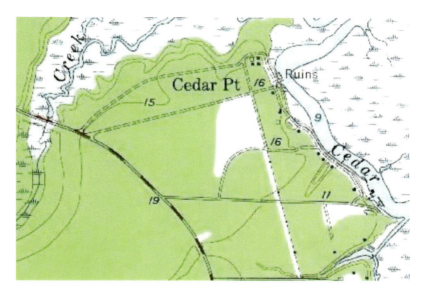

Cedar Point, McIntosh County, in 1954, from a USGS topographical map. The group of four buildings at the top represent the Johnson-Hunter-Sullivan properties, 1911 to present. Many of the other structures in the community shown are still present in 2023, including the venerable Atwood house, the next black square south of our four family dwellings. There are four dirt roads and one paved road shown—the paved one is state highway 99, the old Cow Horn Road, at left as it curves and crosses Cedar Creek at Oak Hill. There was once a saw mill at Oak Hill. The top dirt road leads directly east to the family properties before turning south along Cedar Creek. The next road runs east from 99 to its terminus at the Atwood house (roughly a block south of the family properties) and the abandoned oyster cannery, indicated by "Ruins," on the waterfront. A quarter mile or so south is the improved dirt road from 99 leading to the shrimp docks and Amason ice plant on the creek, with a side lane to the homes of Guy and Shirley Amason, and Laura Campbell. Riverside Drive runs along the creek north to south from the Johnson-Hunter lots to the ice plant. The road at the very bottom of the map leads to Manchester. The two black squares at bottom right indicate the homes (then) of the W.M. Forsyth and Karl Brittain families. All the roads are now paved except the one at the top, which was closed by private land owners ca. 1980, then re-opened in 2021, also as private.

Cedar Point, my ancestral property overlooking the marshes and creek.

Looking west at sunset through Creighton Narrows on the intracoastal waterway. The hammock at far left, created from dredge spoil from the Narrows, was a favored camping spot during my adolescence growing up at Cedar Point, seen in the distance on the mainland. Little has changed here except the hammocks have grown larger. (Aimee G. Gaddis photo)

School house and students at Valona, 1912. The Valona school operated from 1907 to 1917. Pictured on front row l-r: Jane Atwood, Sophie Atwood, Maggie Durant, Mary Durant, Hugh Burrows, Stuart Atwood. Back row: Paul Dunwoody, James Atwood, Alex Durant, Salome Atwood, Claire Burrows, Miss Mattie Buckner, Lewis Burrows, Emma Dunwoody.

Abandoned post office and store, quite possibly the same structure as that in the top image, on the waterfront at Valona adjacent to the old Watson docks—a place oft-visited by the author and his friends and cousins in the 1950s and 1960s. It was built ca. 1900. J.A. Radford and his wife managed the post office and store in the 50s and 60s. Later, Lewis Burrows Graham, a member of the traditional shrimp fishing families of Valona and Cedar Point, served for many years as the last postmaster before the permanent closure of the little post office in 1995 upon her death at age 97.

Cedar Point, north end. Home is about 50 yards away overlooking this marsh.

Whether from the associations of a happy childhood, or from a charm in the scenes themselves, or from a peculiarity of natural taste, my heart clings to the tidewater. To this day, every relic of it interests me. I cannot see, in these mountainous regions where I now dwell, a handful of moss brought from the coast, or see, in the streets of these upland towns, a crimson fragment of crab or prawn; but my pulse quickens at the sight of it, and it makes me almost laugh, on my occasional visits to the coast, to note how the smell of the salt marsh rejoices my olfactories like the perfume of roses. Dear old Seaboard! With your grand expanses of water, your stretches of green waving marsh, your sea birds of endless variety and tireless wing, your waters musical with the flutter of fish, your forests evergreen with magnolia, and live oak and cedar, pine and palmetto, and your groves of orange, and fig, and pomegranate luxuriantly rooted in your rich sands—FAREWELL! I expect to die loving you as at the first; and if ever a kind Providence favors the wish, you shall see me as one of your children again...

Francis R. Goulding, 1870, describing the McIntosh tidewater[1]

To describe growing up in the low country, I would have to take you to the marsh on a spring day, flush the great blue heron from its silent occupation, scatter marsh hens as we sink to our knees in mud, open you an oyster with a pocketknife and feed it to you from the shell and say "There. That taste. That's the taste of my childhood." And I would say, "Breathe deeply" and you would breathe and remember that smell for the rest of your life, the bold, fecund aromas of the tidal salt marsh, exquisite and sensual, the smell of the South in heat, a smell all perfumed with seawater. My heart belongs in the marshlands. The boy in me still carries the memories when I lifted crab pots out of the river before dawn, when I was shaped by life on the river, part child, part sacristan of tides.

Pat Conroy, *The Prince of Tides*[2]

---

[1] Francis R. Goulding, *Sapelo, Or Child-Life on the Tide Water* (1870).
[2] Pat Conroy, *The Prince of Tides* (Boston: Houghton, Mifflin, 1986). Used with permission. Pat Conroy (1945-2016) had a low country upbringing contemporaneous to my own, and we each shared a mutual appreciation for, and understanding of, the coastal ecosystem. He is universally recognized as a leading figure of modern Southern literature.

C oming home...

      Simple words, yet they represent far more than meets the eye in my case.

Truly, I have always been at home wherever I have been in my native tidewater Georgia, but in 2018, I *literally* came home, likely—hopefully—for the last time. Going home is a fundamental instinct all of us have but which, in later life, few of us can ever hope to attain however much we may yearn for it. I am one of the lucky ones. I began at Cedar Point and, God willing, I will end at Cedar Point amid the tides and marshes. It is thus truly a case of a life lived 360 degrees.[3]

    My first conscious memory as a child very likely was that of the smell of the salt marsh at Cedar Point. That thoroughly distinctive aroma must have indelibly—and permanently—etched itself upon my lifelong awareness long before I attained any particular notion of its import or significance.

---

[3] In June 2018 I completed the building of my Cedar Point home on ancestral land and moved from nearby Richmond Hill where I had resided for the previous twenty years. During that time, however, I was employed in McIntosh County at Sapelo Island, and was fully engaged in researching and writing the county's history.

My Cedar Point back yard and palm trees at sunset, with Baisden's Bluff in the distance across the marsh.

I share my affinity for, and memories of, the marshes with an abundance of sentimentality to any and all who will listen to me, whether in my lectures, teaching or casual conversations with family and friends. The salt marshes are inextricably attached to my unending romance with the low country coast, along with its oak, pine and palm forests, the restless dunes of the island beaches, the endless fluidity of the tides and winds, the egrets, herons and pelicans, those and other familiar denizens inhabiting our

The view from home in 2022—my Cedar Point front lawn with the river at high tide beyond, precisely where my great-grandfather Johnson built a two-story house a hundred years earlier.

extraordinary ecosystem. But the ecological signature of our coastal country is undeniably the marshes, and the floods and ebbs of the tides that nurture them.

The late Pat Conroy is almost poetic in evoking the truest sense of the marshes, the aromas and beauty of which quicken the pulse of native coastal Southerners. Like Conroy, my life too was "shaped by life on the river" and I too have always embraced the endless vicissitudes of the marshes with their pervasive aromatic pungency—particularly amid the mudflats at low tide on a warm, languid summer afternoon. There is nothing earthly comparable to the marvelous, majestic marshes of the Georgia and South Carolina low country. Small wonder then, and with no exaggeration, that from an early age we have always called this "God's Country."

I have always encouraged my children to "breathe deeply" and savor the alluring aroma of the marshes. One of the last things I said to my daughter Amanda as she went away to the University of Georgia for her freshman year of college was, "No matter what you do in life, or where you are on this earth, you will always be drawn home by the smell of the salt marsh, and its association with the best memories of your childhood." Eventually, I think we all come back home to the marshes—certainly so in spirit, if not always in reality. We children of the low country always sense the gentle allure of the marshes wherever we are. We are drawn back, somehow wanting to come full circle to reside again amidst the ambient sensuality of our adolescence, to again embrace the securities and remembrances that are uniquely associative to those verdant green blades of *Spartina* that comprise the miracle of the marshes. My children and I get all this honestly. All the generations of our family have experienced similar feelings of the need to be drawn home to the seaboard at various stages in life, myself included, of course. We are infused with the infectious lure of the marshes, the mudflats, the sea and the tides, the blue heron ever in search of the elusive fiddler crab.

The quiet little tidewater settlement of Cedar Point, in McIntosh County in coastal Georgia, was where, in the nineteen fifties and sixties, I spent a great deal of my childhood and adolescence experiencing the supposed affecting innocence of youth. It was also a time when I acquired, through my family and their friends, a growing appreciation for coastal history and culture. Much of the early tradition of the local oyster and shrimp fisheries is related to the Atwood family, descendants of Henry and Ann McIntosh Atwood. Simple advice given by Meta Atwood Watson is as applicable today as it was when she expressed her thoughts in the early 1900s and fits perfectly within the theme of this book: "Never move away from the coast because you'll never starve here," the family matriarch told her children. Her father, John McIntosh Atwood, taught his family equally deep allegiance to the tidewater, but for a different reason— he knew his children might leave temporarily but they would always return to "smell the marshes."

With the acquired—and often painfully gradual—maturity that came in those adolescent years, I found myself embarking on a growing love affair with my native land-and-seascape, amid the pleasant associations of our little tidewater communities and neighbors, all familiar names, some not even on a map—Cedar Point, Crescent, Belleville, Manchester, Valona, Hudson and Meridian, most with sandy roads overlaid with crushed shell that were so hot to one's bare feet in the summer, the coast all buffered by the barrier islands a few miles in the distance—Sapelo, Doboy, Blackbeard and Creighton. In my mind's eye I can still see the greenish-blue tree line of Creighton in the distance, directly across the marsh from Cedar Point, reposing placidly a mile eastward. It was an exposure to which I related many times sitting on the steps of the "big house" at Cedar Point. Creighton was long, low and always to my vivid childhood

Abandoned oyster boats in front of our Cedar Point home in 1959.

imagination looking much like a long passenger train racing along the tracks towards its terminus by the sea. And always the smells, the omnipresent aromas associated with my youth, not only those of the marsh, but also of burning oak leaves in the early spring, deer tongue plants drying in the sun, and the familiar iodine scents experienced around the shrimp docks with their blends of fish and crab, salt air and the mudflats at low tide, these in harmony with the mix of diesel fuel and tarred shrimp nets. There was, and remains, a sublime pleasantness about these olfactory associations of my youth.

I have wonderful childhood and adolescent recollections of Cedar Point—roaring fires, loud conversation and laughter amid a house full of people at Christmas, a rope swing in the big live oak tree out front, swimming in the shallow "tide pool" at the Point, feeding the chickens in the back yard on cold mornings, building a pirate ship out of an old brick barbecue pit, beach excursions to St. Simons and Jekyll with cousins, aunts, uncles and friends; and the memorable occasion in the summer of 1964 when we rode out Hurricane Dora at Cedar Point, with the terrifying wild run of the winds uprooting hundred-year-old live oaks, and the surging waters of the nearby creek rising ever closer to the front doorstep. It was that time span from 1957 through 1967, covering my ages 11 through 20, that were truly the most memorable years of my adolescence. They were the balmy, palmy days of summer in coastal Georgia, carefree, footloose days. We were typical "river rats," as my friends, cousins and I wandered like nomads about Cedar Point and Valona, sometimes with a "plan", but more often than not simply

19

Shellbluff Creek, Valona: The lazy summer days of our youth on the McIntosh County tidewater in the 1950s. (Author's collection)

acting upon the spontaneity and impulses that are the inevitable companions of youth.

Occasionally we would ride our bicycles the 1½ miles along Highway 99 from Cedar Point to Sess Driggers' store at Crescent, for the simple expedient of purchasing a Coke and a nickel bag of salted peanuts. More often than not we could be seen swimming off the dock in the creek at Quiz Forsyth's house at Manchester, impatiently awaiting high tide and slack water—the best time for enjoying the creek; or roaming about the sandy roads of Valona, sometimes crunching through the oyster shell lane leading down to Alex Durant's shrimp docks there on Shellbluff Creek, or purchasing snacks nearby at J.A. Radford's little store and post office. No purpose in mind whatsoever until, spotting (and enjoying the invigorating aromas) the big rusting steel drums full of Atlantic blue crabs caught by the nets of the local boats. We all had the thought simultaneously—let's get some chicken necks, lines and a peach basket and go crabbing. And just like that, three or four of us would be off to Johnny Ream's, or Hunter Watson's, pulling an old pine bateau out of the marsh and pushing it down the muddy bank, off for an afternoon of crabbing in the nearby creek. This often occurred in our ramblings around Cedar Point as well. The constant proximity

Alex Durant's shrimp boat docks, Shellbluff Creek, Valona, circa 1962.

to fresh seafood was like an aphrodisiac—it precipitated a natural inclination to indulge in the bounty of the waters all around us. The aromas of the marshes amid the creeks at low tide, with the hot breath of the July sun bearing on sun-reddened backs, dipping crab lines close to a mud flat, luring the Atlantic blues toward their impending date with a steam pot later that afternoon.

Meeting the incoming shrimp boats in late afternoon was always a highlight. Many were the days I eagerly sprinted down the sandy lane paralleling Cedar Creek to Hugh Burrows' docks to meet Cap'n Bobo (Hugh Burrows) bringing in the *Pinta* from twelve or more hours of trawling in the Sound or offshore of Sapelo. The fragrances of the docks have never left me—a mixture of the smells of nets, dried-out shrimp and fish, salt water and marsh wrack, diesel fuel and tar. As a lad of twelve and thirteen, Bobo paid me fifty cents every Saturday morning to clean the deckhouse of the *Pinta*. Starting in the galley, I hand-washed pots, cutlery, and crockery, including those heavy coffee mugs that were so thick you could almost drive a nail with one; scrubbed down the table and floor, stocked the groceries for the coming week in the cupboards and the below-deck freezer, tidied the stateroom, and swept out and cleaned the windows of the wheelhouse. I'd have done it all for nothing, it was so invigorating. But Bobo always gave me a half-dollar piece (there were

Hugh Burrows' dock, boats, and net house at Cedar Point in 1959. Guy Amason's dock and net house is at far right.

still such things in those days) upon the completion of my labors, and in those days, fifty cents was a small fortune to a kid. For instance, it could cover the Saturday afternoon matinee in Darien with my friends, including a fountain Coke and bag of popcorn.

There was another aspect of my affinity for the local boats and the shrimping industry during my adolescence: actually going out on the boats and experiencing the life firsthand. My first adventure on a shrimp boat occurred in the summer of 1957 at the age of eleven, spending a day on the aging *St. Catherine*, operated by Captain Stuart Atwood of Cedar Point. When Captain Atwood came by to pick me up at 5:00 a.m. my initial reaction was to roll over and go back to sleep. No one in their right mind would start their day at such an ungodly hour. However, my grandmother prodded me awake and said "get ready and go...you will be glad you did." And I was. It was a wonderful experience out on the open sea on a hot, cloudless day, the sky so blue it almost hurt; observing the "striker" handle the nets after each two-hour "drag", emptying the nets on the deck of the vessel's stern; then watching he and Captain Atwood go through the catch, sorting the shrimp into baskets which were iced down and stored in the hold. The day was intoxicating. I was hooked. Validating this were the summer days, out of school with time to burn, over the next few years that I listened raptly on the old vacuum tube radio borrowed from a neighbor, taking in every syllable of the back and forth short-wave small talk between boat captains in Sapelo Sound or off the islands, the unique technical language of the local

22

View from the front porch: sunlight over the marshes toward the islands.

watermen, and the accommodating exchange of information: where
the shrimp were, and weren't, running for instance. It was clear that
the boat captains had a bond. They were thoroughly professional,
completely knowledgeable about their trade, and armed with the
necessary skills and understanding to safely and expediently navigate
the local waters inshore and offshore of McIntosh County.

In subsequent summers I occasionally had the opportunity to
accompany Burrows out on the *Pinta* for all-day shrimping in the
offshore Atlantic waters. These excursions were always memorable,
but we worked hard—Bobo was not into providing pleasure cruises.
You went "fishing" with him, and you earned it. We helped with the
nets, headed shrimp, hosed down the deck between catches, cleaned
the galley and took cat naps on the bow in the warm sunshine during
drags as the long, extended double outriggers towed the nets and the
vessel's powerful Caterpillar diesel engine pulled the accumulating
bags and catch along the sea floor. These trips were always made
enjoyable by the food. The local shrimpers definitely knew how to
eat. Usually the striker prepared breakfast just as dawn broke, and as
the sun rose in the east over the sea horizon, with the first drag of the
morning begun and the two-hour lull before hauling in the nets.
There would be strong, steaming coffee served up in thick crockery

East side of Creighton Island from Front River, part of the intracoastal waterway, and a frequently used route by shrimp boats heading to sea.

mugs with sugar and canned milk, hot grits and butter, scrambled eggs, with ham or bacon. Lunch came in the early afternoon, and was often shrimp creole, prepared with shrimp that had been in the ocean an hour earlier, simmered in a thick, rich-and-spicy, made-from-scratch, perfectly-seasoned tomato sauce with onion, bell pepper, a dash or two of oregano, the blend served over a bed of hot white rice—with sweet iced tea to wash it down. It was a grand, almost romantic sort of life for us, but we determined early on that it was not going to be permanent for us. Shrimp fishing was the hardest kind of work imaginable—laborious, tedious, and monotonous—with seemingly little to show for it except for torn nets, constant engine repairs, and occasionally becoming grounded on uncharted sandbars. But I will always remember the *Pinta*, with its high peaked bow, sleek lines, her tall outriggers, the deep muffled hum of its engines, the clouds of sea gulls trailing her wake swooping into the water for fish morsels and other unwanted species tossed over the side while the shrimp catch was being sorted. They were the best of summer days for a child of the coast, experiences never to be forgotten, always to be as warmly remembered as the soft azure sunshine off the sea.

I loved the shrimping communities of Valona and Cedar Point in the days of my youth, they being two small settlements of about fifty or so residents each where the head of each family, and others, was associated in some way with the commercial fishery—most as boat owners and captains. The 1950s and the 1960s were the heyday of these communities when the boats were numerous and the shrimp takes at their greatest—this was long before the late 70s when rising fuel prices and the undercutting competition of foreign imported shrimp began to lead to a serious downturn in the southeast Atlantic

24

fishery. I was glad to have witnessed the peak of this activity, as I have described in detail in the preceding pages. Years later, in the late 1980s while doing research for my history of McIntosh County, *Early Days on the Georgia Tidewater*, I consulted the estimable Lewis Graham, then the matriarch of the Valona-Cedar Point fishing families, for her recollections of those heady days when the industry was thriving.

Lewis (Burrows) Graham (1898-1995) of Cedar Point, sister of Hugh Burrows and Hunter Watson, and perhaps best remembered for her many years of service as Valona postmaster, recalled the peak years of shrimping in McIntosh County, a livelihood with which she always had a close connection. She experienced two generations of family shrimpers, and shared her memories with the author in 1989:

"They were wonderful days. The days of shrimp fishing when it really meant something in this county. Hugh and Hunter, and all the others, worked awfully hard. They had to work hard to become the successes they were in the local shrimping business. In the early days, the boats stayed out only one day at a time. They didn't have the advantage then of having ice on board to keep their catch cool. Hunter and Hugh and the others would go out in the boats—and they were little boats then—at daybreak. The boats were so small some didn't have a deckhouse. They would haul in their nets by hand, which was terribly hard work. The shrimpers made their coffee and boiled shrimp to eat in little sandbox fires they made on the decks of their boats. They would come home exhausted at the end of the day. Someone on shore would always keep an eye out for the boats in the late afternoon. When the boats were sighted on their way in, someone would drive to Meridian or Crescent or wherever, and pick up the headers. The shrimp would have to be headed and sent out as soon as the boats returned in the late afternoon or the shrimp would spoil. A lot of the heading was done right on the boats on the way in. Valona and Cedar Point were the big ports for the shrimp boats. They always have been—except for Darien, which always had a lot of boats tied up on both sides of the bridge. The creeks going to Valona and Cedar Point out of the sounds were among the few that were deep enough for the shrimpers to use on the lowest tides. Later, the boats started getting bigger. Men began to own more than one boat. The blacks and whites worked together in the industry here and helped each other. Hugh Burrows had all those boats and docks along the creek at Cedar Point. His finest boat was the *Pinta*, 57 feet and about 30 tons, built in the late 1950s. She was the beauty of all the McIntosh County shrimp boats. The *Pinta* was the boat Hugh fished himself, but he had several others.[32] Two of them were the *Franchel* and the *Gaius*, both about 45 feet. Hunter Watson had his own docks at Valona there on the creek across the way from Alex Durant's docks. In the 1950s and 60s, like Hugh, he was at the top of his profession. One of his bigger boats was the *Chief*. It fitted him. He also had the *Mar-Gin*, and the *Adventure*, both close to sixty feet. Those were all wonderful boats. But the biggest shrimp boat anybody had ever seen hereabouts up to that time was probably the *Miss Valona*, a big 62-footer, which Mr. [J.A.] Radford, who ran the store at Valona, had built about 1959 or 1960."

Darien and McIntosh County have long had a maritime tradition, one which began in the colonial era, then came to full flower in the antebellum period with Darien's rise as a prominent cotton, rice and timber market, and the water-borne flow of plantation commodities along the inland waterway to the larger towns. People relied on the waterways for mobility, roads being of poor quality and connection before the arrival of railroads and, then later, highways. Boats of all sizes and description were to be found on the waters of tidewater Georgia and lower South Carolina. Boat builder and small-craft historian Rusty Fleetwood of Tybee Island in his book *Tidecraft* said it best: "To tell the story of this region, it is necessary to tell of boats. Not necessarily fancy or large craft, just plain, get-from-here-to-there boats that could live with the mud, the oyster rakes, the narrow creeks, and the short, choppy seas of the sounds and would be simple and cheap to build and operate." I understood this at a very early age, obviously due to my proximity to tidal waters and shrimp fishermen and my own explorations on the local creeks and rivers, blessedly free from the constraints and diversions of "the hill"—the high ground of our environment.

This was thus a time when my curiosity and interest in our coastal geography manifested itself. By the age of twelve I was devouring the Coast and Geodetic Survey navigational charts of local waters. I also had topographic and hydrologic maps of our land and water areas spread over the floor and table where I memorized every place name, learned every nuance of the waterways, the tidal ranges, the location and movement of sandbars, shoals and mudflats, and the depths of the creeks we regularly explored in our little pine bateau. These investigations awakened my historical awareness, and a growing

Shrimp boats at Darien at the time Quiz Forsyth and I catalogued them in 1959, with the boats at Valona and Cedar Point. (Author's collection)

interest in learning more. The abandoned oyster factory and docks in front of my grandmother's house at Cedar Point were always a source of interest. This operation thrived in the 1930s and 40s, and here my father and two friends managed affairs during the period right after World War II. There were a couple of summers when Quiz Forsyth and I cataloged the names and owners of all the shrimp boats at Valona, Cedar Point, Belleville and Meridian. We cycled to the docks in these communities, plus hitch-hiked into Darien several times, to compile our lists of the boats there, and even sketch pictures of the boats on ruled notebook paper, however crude and amateurish these drawings turned out to be looking back on them now. The ballast islands along the waterways near the sounds were always intriguing to me. Often, in the four summers from 1960 through 1963, I made solo exploratory forays by boat to these areas, taking notes and photographs of such places as Hazzard's ballast pile, Creighton, Doboy and Commodore islands, the old lighthouse on the tip of Sapelo, Hird Island, the tabby ruins on Carnochan Creek at the Thicket, and the shrimp docks at Meridian, Valona, Cedar Point and Belleville. There were many excursions in my little aluminum boat with the 10-horsepower Evinrude kicker, going from Cedar Point to Valona, cutting through the marsh on high tide to Kittles docks on the lower tip of Valona, down Atwood Creek past Patterson Island, thence to Doboy Sound and Blue and Hall. All these trips were south of Cedar Point. I made other forays to the

Hazzard's ballast island on Front River, near the entrance (at right) to Sapelo Sound. In childhood days we occasionally fished and crabbed here and explored amid the ballast stones deposited by overseas timber ships in the late 1800s. There was a free-flowing artesian well at Hazzard's, an endless source of fresh water. The well stopped flowing due to the opening of the paper mill at Riceboro, twenty miles north.

north, along the Crescent River to Creighton and Baisden's Bluff, Belleville, via Rattlesnake Cut, then to Pine Harbor and Fairhope via Roscoe's Cut that connected both sides of Belleville on the Sapelo River. As river rats we spent a lot of summer time in those days around Belleville, Pine Harbor, Cedar Point and Valona water skiing, camping out on small marsh hammocks, casting for shrimp and crabbing. We never thought we'd ever grow up—or needed to—and thus have to give up those carefree days on the river amid the tides.[4]

Years later, when my children were still young, I realized the urges had never waned, the pull of the water was just as intense as ever. We graduated to a bigger craft, and the girls and I made longer trips—to exotic, isolated places like Blackbeard and Cabretta islands, going "outside" and navigating south along the shores of Sapelo, going swimming on the south tip of Nanny Goat Beach with the abandoned lighthouse tower across the way on sparkling sunlit summer afternoons. Then there were my serious historical investigations by water to the Darien River, the rice islands of the

---

[4] The next chapter includes an account of my adolescent waterway explorations, and my perspectives on our local waterways later in life.

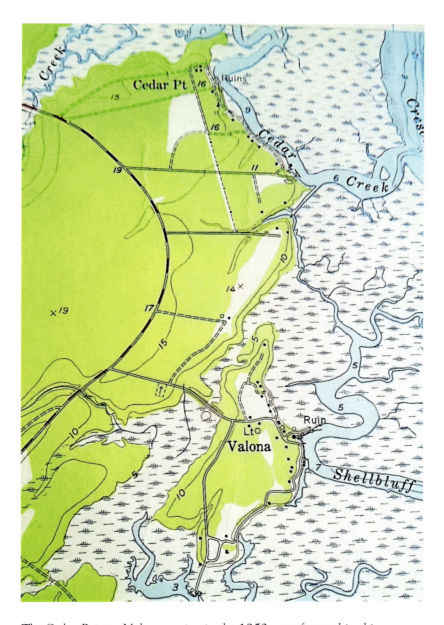

The Cedar Point-to-Valona section in the 1950s as referenced in this memoir. Dirt roads lead in to (top to bottom) Cedar Point, Manchester, Todd Field, and Valona. Shown are houses, docks, marshes, waterways and uplands. This is our neighborhood from my childhood and adolescence.

Altamaha delta—Butler's Island, Cambers Island, Hammersmith Creek, Altama and the abandoned rice canals of Broughton and Elizafield—then northward into Sapelo Sound to the ballast islands along Front River, and across the Sound to Julianton on the south end of Harris Neck. It was important to me to be able to physically "experience" the locales I was writing about in my history books. Along the same lines were the many auto trips to the remotest sections of the county, such as the Harris Neck wildlife refuge, Jones, Townsend, Cox and the long-abandoned settlements of Warsaw and Ninety Four, all tucked away amid the pine flatwoods of western McIntosh County.

* * *

Both the maternal and paternal sides of my family have South Carolina roots. My father's Sullivan-Sumner forebears migrated from Virginia, and North and South Carolina, eventually to Lee and Worth counties in South Georgia, in the late 1700s and early 1800s. I am one of five generations on my mother's side of our family to either reside in, or be born and reared in, McIntosh County. My maternal great-grandfather, Thomas M. Hunter of South Carolina, came to coastal Georgia in 1894 when he became the pastor of the Darien Presbyterian Church.

My maternal grandfather, Howard O. Hunter (1895-1964), was born at Ashantilly, near Darien, during his father's Presbyterian pastorate. My mother, Mary Kate Hunter Sullivan, born in 1924 in Macon, grew up in McIntosh County. I was born in Savannah (1946), and my children, Kenneth Patrick, born in Columbus (1971), Teri, born in LaGrange (1978), and Amanda Kate, born in Savannah (1983), gives us five generations of residence in, or being native to coastal Georgia.

The pulpit vacancy of the Darien Presbyterian Church in early 1894, accounts for my family's coastal Georgia roots. Thomas Hunter, just out of Seminary, was called to this church in July 1894, where he began a three-year record in his first full-time pastorate. The church is a beautiful Gothic-Victorian edifice nestled amid a spreading live oak canopy, with the grounds covered with azaleas that burst forth in an explosion of bloom in the spring. My first foray into writing about coastal history was occasioned by the 250th anniversary of this, my legacy church.

The congregation was established in 1736 by Scottish Highlanders upon the founding of the town of Darien during the early years of the Georgia colony, making the church the oldest Presbyterian congregation in Georgia. The church edifice in 1894 was on the same spot upon which the present church reposes. However, the wood church built in 1876 accidentally burned in 1899, after the Hunters had departed Darien, and the present tabby and masonry church was built in 1900, completed in just over a year after the fire. In the present church, there are twenty-one memorial pews, which have been in place since 1940. A number of these bear the inscribed brass plates of members of the Hunter-Johnson-Sullivan family. One of them commemorates the service of Thomas and Sallie Hunter during his 1894-97 pastorate; another bears the name of my mother, Mary Kate, her mother, Mary Jackson Hunter, and her brother, H. Owen Hunter, Jr. My children are the fifth generation of our family to have either grown up in, or been closely affiliated with, the Darien Presbyterian Church.

Besides Georgia, my maternal and paternal ancestries have generational ties to Virginia, North and South Carolina, and Tennessee. In my personal papers there is a letter relating some Sullivan family genealogy from Pastor Bryan C. Sullivan (1941-) of Elgin, Texas, written to me in 1993, that states, in part, "The more that I research the Sullivan families of coastal and southern Georgia the more I believe that they are all related to each other. I believe that I will eventually show that they all came from only one or two ancestors from South Carolina. It does appear, however, that they entered Georgia at somewhat different times and by different routes. I think that the Sullivant (Sillevant) family which came with the early settlers to Midway, Liberty County, Georgia, are some of our people. They were inter-married with the Normans, Frasers, Singletons, Spencers, etc."

Diligent research among available records for our family by Alcye L. Sullivan shows that John Thomas Sullivan (1637-1678) was likely our earliest direct-line Sullivan ancestor in North America, migrating from Ireland to Virginia as early as the 1670s, where a son, Owen Sullivan (I), was born in 1679. Our line of Sullivans was in South Carolina by the 1750s, migrating there from Virginia. There, Owen Sullivan (III) had a son, William Sullivan, Sr. (1755-1840). William Sullivan was apparently the first of our Sullivans to live in Georgia since records show that his only child, William Sullivan, Jr., was born in Washington, Georgia, in 1790. This family relocated to Lee County, Georgia where William, Sr. and his wife, Mary Brantley Sullivan, both died in 1840. The son of William Sullivan, Jr., William Manning Sullivan, was born in Lee County in 1828. The thread of my family ties to South Georgia is a strong and interesting one and remains so. I have vivid childhood memories of interaction with my Sullivan-Sumner South Georgia forebears.[5]

My father, Roy Earl Sullivan (1921-2016) was born January 14th, 1921 in Sumner, Worth County, Georgia. Sumner is a little village, unincorporated, on US Highway 82 about halfway between Albany and Tifton in the heart of South Georgia. My father's parents, Harvey LeRoy (Roy) and Willie Lemon Sullivan, were both from close-knit South Georgia communities. Roy was from Decatur County, on the Georgia-Florida state line, and Willie was a native of Worth County.

Harvey Leroy Sullivan (1893-1967), my paternal grandfather, was one of twelve children born to Henry Wilburn Sullivan (1860-1943) and Ellen Ethel Holt Sullivan (1862-1935). Henry Sullivan was the son of William Manning Sullivan (1828-1883), who was born in Leesburg, Georgia, and died in Camilla, Mitchell County, Georgia. William M. Sullivan's wife was Rebecca Jane Shiver (1827-1912). Henry (born 1860) was one of six children born to them in Camilla.

Henry W. Sullivan became a Baptist minister, which makes for an interesting coincidence as two of my great-grandfathers were ordained ministers, Henry Sullivan on the paternal side, and Thomas Hunter on the maternal. Henry and Ellen Sullivan lived much of their lives in Bainbridge, Decatur County, where Henry preached at a church in the nearby small town of Whigham. The families of both William M. Sullivan and his son Henry W. Sullivan are buried in Mt. Pleasant Cemetery in Vada, Georgia, on the boundary line between Decatur and Mitchell counties.

Wilma Frances (Willie) Lemon Sullivan (1900-1986), my paternal grandmother, was a Sumner by lineage, the Sumners being among the earliest families of the South. Our line of Sumners evolved from North Carolina, eventually migrating to Emanuel County in southeast Georgia after the American Revolution, later settling in Worth County. This family has military bearing: Sumners served in the Revolution; my great-great-great grandfather, Joseph M. Sumner, was an officer in the Confederate army, and both my father (Second World War and Korea) and paternal grandfather (First World War) served in the U.S. Army.

---

[5] Useful printed sources of information about this section are Folks Huxford, ed., *Pioneers of Wiregrass Georgia*, vol. 5 (1967), and Lillie M. Grubbs, *History of Worth County, Georgia, 1854-1934* (1934).

The first Sumner for which I have a record is William Sumner, born in 1665, and who we know was in the Virginia colony as early as 1691. The earliest Sumner we know of in Georgia was Joseph Sumner, Sr. (1761-1827), died and buried in Emanuel County, Georgia. Joseph Sumner, Jr. (1793-1880) married Mahala Smith (1799-1882) in 1813 in Emanuel County. They are the first Sumners to settle in the settlement that bears their name in Worth County. Both are buried in the Sumner family cemetery just outside Sumner. The Confederate Army veteran was their son, Joseph Milton Sumner (1836-1913), one of seventeen children, whose wife was Jane Young Sumner (1841-1930). Their daughter, Frances Nell Sumner (1865-1940) married Malcolm Currie Lemon (1855-1901) of Sumner. To this couple was born my grandmother in 1900, Wilma (Willie) Lemon. Willie married Harvey Leroy Sullivan in January 1920 in Worth County, and my father was born at Sumner in early 1921. Willie died October 1, 1986 in Columbus and is buried with my grandfather Roy (died December 22, 1967) in Tifton, Georgia, where the couple lived for many years. Their home was at 410 West 6th Street, close to Eve Park where my grandfather Sullivan often took me to see baseball games played by the local minor league Class D team.

My maternal great-grandfather, Rev. Dr. Thomas Marshall Hunter (1870-1937), son of Miles Hill Hunter (1834-1914) and Sallie Marshall Hunter (1847-1891), was born April 7, 1870, at Chester, South Carolina. He earned his college degree at The Citadel in Charleston, and his theological training at Southwestern Presbyterian College Seminary (now Austin Peay State University) in Clarkesville, Tennessee, graduating in the spring of 1894. My great-grandfather Hunter took the first steps toward a lifelong career in the Presbyterian ministry as he filled a pastorate at the Hermitage Church in Nashville, Tennessee during the last two years of his studies at seminary. During his matriculation at Southwestern Seminary, Hunter became enamored of a local girl, Miss Sallie Owen of Clarkesville. After a suitable courtship, Thomas and Sallie were married in Clarkesville in November 1894 at the time he had just accepted his call to the Darien Presbyterian Church. Sallie Owen and her sisters, Kate and Mary, were all born in Clarkesville, Tennessee, the daughters of Lebanon, Tennessee native Benjamin Howard Owen (1849-1940), a druggist, and Mary Beta Kennedy Bryan (1851-1924). Kate and Mary both married sons of South Carolina families,

Rev. Dr. Thomas Marshall Hunter in his later years.

the Ravenels and the Geers, and lived in Charleston, where their father died in 1940.

The Charleston connection has grown in my awareness in recent years, stimulated in part by my daughter Amanda's marriage in November 2007 at historic St. Michael's Episcopal Church in Charleston to Hugh McColl Wilson, Jr., of a long-established Charleston medical family; this event naturally precipitated my spending greater amounts of time in and around the city. My daughter's own research shows that our Charleston forebears were true "South of Broad" people: Mary Owen (my great aunt) and her husband, Andrew Geer, lived at 2 Gibbes Street, near the Charleston Battery, and Kate Owen (another great aunt, and sister of Sallie and Mary), and her husband, Willie Bee Ravenel, resided at 135 Tradd Street, not far from Legare Street, the latter apparently named for a family around which much of my research has evolved—i.e. see my *Darien Journal of John Girardeau Legare.*

To summarize, my maternal great-grandmother and two great aunts were the three Owen sisters: Sallie Owen (1872-1959) married my great-grandfather Thomas M. Hunter (1870-1937), Mary Owen (1883-1969) married Andrew Jackson Geer (1865-1943) of Charleston, and Kate Owen (1887-1976) married William Bee Ravenel (1882-1959) of Charleston. It was for my great-aunts, Mary Geer and Kate Ravenel, that my mother, Mary Kate Hunter Sullivan was named, and for her that my youngest child, Amanda Kate, was named. Mary Owen Geer's only child, Benjamin Owen Geer (1907-1992) of Charleston, and Kate Ravenel's only child, William Bee Ravenel, Jr. (1914-1968), were contemporaries, cousins, of my maternal grandfather, Howard Owen Hunter. Hunter and his son, H.O. Hunter, Jr., my mother's brother, were also given the Owen family name.

During Rev. Hunter's pastorate in Darien, Thomas and Sallie resided for a time at Ashantilly, an old residence just outside Darien built by Thomas Spalding in the early 1800s. There is a connectivity to all this for me personally. Spalding, of Ashantilly and Sapelo Island, is the focus of my research and writing a century after my great-grandparents resided in that house. My sense of connection to Ashantilly is evoked in my research and writing of its history. The revelation that Thomas and Sallie Hunter lived at Ashantilly came to me during my research pursuant to my book, *The Darien Journal of John Girardeau Legare, Ricegrower*. Legare, who cultivated rice on General's Island near Darien, was a friend of the Hunters, a ruling elder of the Presbyterian Church, and resided in the Ashantilly settlement near the Hunters. He noted in his journal in late 1894 that the Ashantilly house was being rented by the new pastor of the Darien Presbyterian Church. Adjacent to Ashantilly is the local cemetery, St. Andrew, where repose my mother, Mary Kate, my grandmother Mary Hunter, and my great-grandmother, Wilhelmina Wheeler Johnson. Thomas Hunter's pastorate occurred during a time of great prosperity for Darien, when the town was the leading processor and shipper of yellow pine timber on the U.S. east coast. In the 1890s Darien was much as it is now—a small, compact, close-knit community. The Hunters had a child during their Darien sojourn. On July 25, 1895, my grandfather, Howard Owen Hunter, was born at Ashantilly, which fact provides yet another personal connection between myself and Ashantilly about which I would write so much, and its builder Thomas Spalding. After leaving Darien, T.M. and Sallie Hunter had a second child, a daughter, Sallie Marshall Hunter (1898-1973), another of my great-aunts. She married J.O. Peery of New Orleans, and lived for many years in Baton Rouge, La.

The Hunters departed Darien in 1897. Thomas served a church in Trenton, Tennessee, for seven years, following which Dr. Hunter pastored one of the largest Presbyterian churches in the South, at Baton Rouge, for eighteen years. Thus, both Howard Hunter, my grandfather, and his sister Marshall, spent much of their adolescence around Baton Rouge and nearby New Orleans. In 1921, Dr. Hunter accepted a call, his last, to pastor the newly organized Westminster Presbyterian Church in Beaumont, Texas. He had a long and distinguished career in the ministry, becoming a prominent member of the Presbyterian ruling hierarchy, and serving as a scholar and minister of the church nationally, Moderator of the Presbyterian Synod of Baton Rouge, and a director of the Austin Theological Seminary. Rev. Hunter died in Beaumont in September 1937 after serving the Westminster Church for fifteen years. He was buried in Baton Rouge. Sallie Owen Hunter died in December 1959, in Baton Rouge where she lived after 1937 with her daughter Marshall Peery, and is buried there beside her husband.[6]

In 1917, H.O. Hunter graduated with honors from Louisiana State University in Baton Rouge. He briefly served in the army in Europe during the First World War, then in 1919, became the regional director of the Boy Scouts of America for the southeastern states, being based in Macon, Georgia. He held this position until 1926. It was in Macon, in December 1920, that my grandfather married my grandmother, Mary Jackson of Macon, daughter by adoption (unsubstantiated) of Dr. Henry Herbert Johnson and Wilhelmina Wheeler Johnson.

---

[6] Much of the preceding material is based on notes from conversations with Edna McNabb Hunter Eller (1913-2004), second wife of Howard O. Hunter. The late Mrs. Eller, my step-grandmother, left to me many of my grandfather's papers, from which was found information relating to his father, T.M. Hunter. The spelling of the Christian name of my great-grandmother has been noted as both "Sallie" and "Sally". I have opted for "Sallie" here, being assured by Edna Eller that Sallie with the "ie" is correct. Edna McNabb was actually my grandfather's third wife. Following his divorce from my grandmother, Mary Jackson Hunter in 1933, H.O. Hunter was married for several years to Marjory Lichty of Pittsburgh, Pa., of whom I have been unable to find information. There is only one reference to her that I have found among the H.O. Hunter papers in my possession, that being a notation in a newspaper article about my grandfather in early 1941.

From this point, Howard Hunter's story becomes a most interesting one indeed, as he came to prominence during a time of national and international tension and crisis precipitated by economic depression and war. From 1926 to 1931, likely due to his successful energies in managing the affairs of the Boy Scouts of America, Hunter served as the administrator of the national Community Chest organization. In 1931, he was made New England director of President Herbert Hoover's Committee on Unemployment and Relief, a significant appointment coming as it did in the wake of the Wall Street crash of October 1929, and the ensuing Depression. By this time, Hunter had established a reputation in government circles for efficiency and diligence in various arenas of civil service and had, not insignificantly, also become a key player in the political machinery of the national Democratic Party.

My grandfather attained higher levels in public service during the administration of Franklin Delano Roosevelt who was elected president in 1932. In 1933, upon beginning his initiative to start the United States' economy on the road to recovery, Roosevelt approved the appointment of Howard Hunter as the Assistant Administrator of the Federal Works and Relief Administration in Washington. Hunter, working out of Chicago, was placed in supervision of work relief programs in the Midwest.

In early 1939, Hunter was named Deputy Commissioner of the Federal Work Projects Administration (WPA), on the occasion of Harry L. Hopkins departing as WPA Commissioner, and the appointment of Francis C. Harrington to succeed him.[7] By then it was obvious that Hunter's star was ascending in Washington political and administrative circles. He had become prominent in national government, a trend that continued for the remainder of the Depression and World War II years. Hunter was named acting Commissioner of the WPA in the fall of 1940, being confirmed for the full appointment by the U.S. Senate in the spring of 1941.

The following newspaper notice announcing these developments is in my grandfather's papers:

---

[7] The Works Progress Administration of 1933 and its successor, the Work Projects Administration, are one and the same. The agency acquired the latter designation under the provisions of FDR's Reorganization Act of April 25, 1939. See Samuel L. Rosenman, ed., *The Public Papers and Addresses of Franklin D. Roosevelt.*

"President Nominates Hunter to be WPA Commissioner--Howard O. Hunter, acting Work Projects Commissioner since the death of Col. F.C. Harrington last September 30, was announced yesterday by President Roosevelt to the rank of WPA Commissioner. A resident of Illinois, Hunter has spent the last 20 years in social work. He was one of the first officials to join in administering the New Deal's relief effort and advanced to his present position through the ranks. Born in Georgia, he moved to Louisiana at an early age and attended Louisiana State University. He enlisted in the Army in 1917 and saw service overseas...When President Roosevelt took office in 1933 and began attacking the unemployment problem by means of the Federal Emergency Relief Administration, Hunter joined that agency at the outset. He served in Chicago as regional director for FERA, later for the Civil Works Administration and still later for the WPA. As regional WPA director he had charge of 13 Midwestern states. This territory included the largest WPA employment of any region in the country. In recognition of this fact Hunter was raised to the rank of assistant commissioner. When drought struck in 1934, Hunter took charge of drought relief in the West and Midwest, and again during the 1936 drought. He directed emergency relief for flood sufferers when the Ohio and upper Mississippi rivers burst their banks in the 1937 flood. In 1939, Hunter was appointed deputy commissioner of the WPA, a month after Col. Harrington became commissioner."[8]

The appointment apparently carried with near-unanimous approval, exemplified by comments in a letter to my grandfather from Justice Frank Murphy, a member of the United States Supreme Court: "My Dear Howard: Not alone because you are a competent public servant and that thus far you have acquitted yourself of your duties in so highly-successful a way, but also because you have a capacity for staunch friendship that I congratulate you on your appointment. That you will do this new errand in the public interest I haven't the least doubt..."[9]

As head of the WPA Hunter supervised, among various other programs, the Federal Writers Project, which not only provided research work for thousands of writers (including many historians) but gave a nation perhaps its first truly comprehensive survey of state and community history through the production of hundreds of books and papers, including the well-received American Guide

---

[8] *Washington Post,* March 11, 1941, p. 3.
[9] Justice Frank Murphy to H.O. Hunter, March 11, 1941, Howard O. Hunter papers, in possession of the author.

Series, books that detailed all 48 states during the time the series was issued in the 1940s and early 1950s.

At this point it is worth noting some examples of the interactions my grandfather had with the President and various administration officials in those critical years of American history, embracing both the Great Depression and the Second World War. The letters of these officials reflect both the energy and the urgency of the times— the participants were simultaneously living and making history, and they all were clearly aware of it. Typical of the correspondence between Howard Hunter and the President is this 1941 note on White House stationery, in my possession, signed by FDR:

"Dear Howard:~That is very generous of you to say about Mr. MacDougall, but while he may be all that you say, his qualifications to run the WPA are not as good as your own. I know of all the sacrifices you have made since 1933, but yours has been a splendid record in every way, and I personally want very much to send your name to the Senate as Administrator and have you continue the fine work that is being done. My best wishes to you, as ever always, Franklin D. Roosevelt."[10]

Since 1938 the U.S. defense establishment had gradually been gathering momentum, even before war erupted on the European continent in September 1939. Millions of Americans were finding employment in the shipyards on three coasts as the U.S. Navy entered a period of rapid growth and expansion. Building the fleet that fought and won a two-ocean war, one that would emerge as the most powerful Navy in world history, was on the building ways in shipyards on three coasts of America, providing the jobs that ultimately brought the nation out of the Depression.[11] On December

---

[10] FDR to H.O. Hunter, March 7, 1941, Howard O. Hunter papers.

[11] Besides naval warships, a massive building effort was underway before and during the war by the U.S. Maritime Commission to construct troop transports that came to be known as Liberty ships. These vessels carried military personnel to the European and Pacific war fronts. Many succumbed to the depredations of German submarines, but America built the ships far faster than they could be sunk, and thus won the war of attrition at sea. Eight-five Liberty ships were constructed at the J.A. Jones shipyard in Brunswick, employing thousands of workers, mostly women and men too old for military service. Some were from Darien and McIntosh County. Other Liberty ships were built at Savannah and yards all along the east and gulf coasts. I have often lectured on this unique aspect of coastal Georgia history, and the contributions of coastal Georgians on the home front.

7, 1941 the Japanese Imperial Navy attacked the U.S. Pacific Fleet at Pearl Harbor, and other military installations on Oahu, Hawaii, and the next day, when Roosevelt asked for a declaration of war against Japan, Howard Hunter issued the following "Night Telegram" to all state Work Projects administrators across the nation:

"December 8, 1941. State of war demands complete cooperation and effectiveness of WPA. War and Navy departments have requested acceleration of work on vital projects and possible deferment of others not essential at this time. You are instructed to close off as rapidly as possible all construction projects of non-defense nature using critical materials or labor where they can be effectively used in defense activity. WPA employment quotas are subject to adjustment if defense requirements indicate. I have offered services of entire administrative staff to War and Navy departments for any local assistance necessary. (Signed) Howard O. Hunter, Commissioner."[12]

Due to the exigencies of America's entry into the world war, the role of the WPA became greatly diminished. By the first part of 1942, soon after the entry of the United States in World War II, the days of the WPA were clearly numbered, as evidenced in the following note from President Roosevelt to Hunter:

"Dear Howard: I regret very much your decision to sever your connection with the Work Projects Administration. Only those of us who have been in the thick of the struggle to establish and maintain an adequate program of work relief can appreciate your part in this effort. Since the inception of the program your advice and support have been heavily relied on by your predecessors and by me. Now that nine years of association is terminating, I want you to know that I appreciate the fine work you have done."[13]

Hunter clearly made a significant contribution to the affairs of government during the Depression and World War II. He played a key role in getting Americans back to work and, concomitantly, did much to improve the nation's infrastructure. Those who are cognizant of such contributions, and whose job it is to preserve the records of such contributions, even from those in the huge federal bureaucracy who largely toil in anonymity away from the direct scrutiny of the public, understand the value of this. Shortly after

---

[12] Memorandum from H.O. Hunter, December 8, 1941, Howard O. Hunter papers, author's collection.
[13] Howard O. Hunter papers, author's collection.

Hunter's death in 1964, his widow, Edna M. Hunter, received the following letter from the Roosevelt Library in Hyde Park, New York:

"Dear Mrs. Hunter: I read a few weeks ago of your husband's death and I would like to express my sympathy to you and your family. Here at the Library we are, of course, familiar with Mr. Hunter's distinguished career in the Federal Emergency Relief Administration and the Works Progress Administration. From Mr. Hunter's extensive correspondence with Mr. Hopkins (whose papers are now in this Library), we know too of the high esteem in which Mr. Hunter was held by leaders of the Roosevelt Administration. As you may know, it was President Roosevelt's hope that persons prominent in his administrations would add their papers to his, so that this Library would become an important research center for the history of this period. Many have already done so...Mr. Hunter's intimate connection with two agencies that played so important a part in the first years of the Roosevelt administrations would make especially appropriate the deposit of his papers here."[14]

Hunter was a private consultant in Washington in administration and public relations from 1943 to 1949 and worked with such agencies as the War Production Board consequent upon America's industrial effort during World War II, the War Food Administration, and the Federal Security Administration. Hunter's papers contain correspondence with President Harry Truman, who succeeded to the presidency in April 1945 upon the death of President Roosevelt at Warm Springs, Georgia. Typical is this note from President Truman to my grandfather, after he assumed office:

"My dear Howard: I appreciate to the full that exceedingly kind letter you sent me. What you say has touched me deeply and you have my real gratitude for your assurance of confidence and support. My warmest thanks for your good wishes for the tasks ahead. Very sincerely yours, Harry Truman." [The president added a handwritten postscript that read: "Sorry to have been so long answering. But there is no time to do anything."][15]

---

[14] Letter dated March 17, 1964 to Mrs. Howard O. Hunter from Elizabeth B. Drewry, Director, Franklin D. Roosevelt Library, Hyde Park, N.Y., National Archives and Records Administration. Original in Hunter papers.
[15] Harry S. Truman to H.O. Hunter, May 16, 1945, Howard O. Hunter papers, author's collection. The postscript was a reference to the president's effort in bringing World War II to a successful conclusion—Germany had surrendered a little over a week before this note was written, and full attention was now being given to completing the effort against Japan in the Pacific, achievement of which occurred several months later, in August.

In 1945, during my grandfather's civil service with the war boards in Washington, he married Edna McNabb (1913-2004), a native of Dothan, Alabama.[16]

During his work with the War Food Administration, M. Lee Marshall of the Continental Baking Company gained my grandfather's acquaintance; it was partly as a result of that friendship that resulted in Hunter accepting a position with the American Institute of Baking (AIB) in 1949. Hunter went to the AIB as executive vice president, and among his first duties was the supervision of the construction of a new headquarters for the Institute in downtown Chicago, Illinois. In 1951, my grandfather was elected president of the Institute, a post he held until his retirement in 1963. During the period of his leadership, the Institute saw sustained growth—the membership of allied industrial corporations and individuals went from fewer than 70 to more than 230. Prior to my grandfather's retirement, leaders in government, science, education and the baking industry gathered in Chicago (October 1963) to acknowledge his achievements during a lifetime of service in both the public and private sectors. A highlight of this occasion was the presentation to Mr. Hunter of a handsome bound volume of letters from his colleagues, associates and friends in many fields.[17]

The Hunters resided on Chicago's North Side during his years as president of the American Institute of Baking. During the 1950s and early 1960s, Hunter maintained his active role in Democratic national politics having frequent interaction with many of the national political figures of the era. An example of this is seen in this note from Truman to my grandfather in the late 1950s:

"Dear Howard: You do not know how very much I appreciated your note of the 16th. You are always on the beam. Your check for $100 is being forwarded to the Hon. John W. McCormack, who is the working chairman of the Matt Connelly Dinner committee. I hope that the next time I am in Chicago you and I will have a chance to visit."[18]

Hunter and his wife Edna were no doubt pleased about the election of the young John F. Kennedy to the presidency in

---

[16] His third marriage. See note 6.

[17] In the Howard O. Hunter papers, author's collection.

[18] Harry S. Truman to H.O. Hunter, June 18, 1959, Howard O. Hunter papers.

November 1960 following his closely won electoral victory over Richard M. Nixon. Among my grandfather's papers is an engraved invitation from the Democratic National Committee requesting the Hunters' presence at the "Inaugural Gala" on January 19, 1961, "In honor of the President-elect of the United States and Mrs. Kennedy", in Washington.[19]

One of the most interesting friendships Hunter and Edna formed was that of the California writer, novelist and future Nobel laureate, John Steinbeck (1902-1968) and his wife, Elaine. The two couples often travelled together and spent much time in Chicago, New Orleans, and other places around the U.S. There is considerable correspondence between my grandfather and Steinbeck among the Hunter papers in my possession. Steinbeck, of course, was best known for his novels depicting ordinary people during the Great Depression, including two classics, *The Grapes of Wrath* and *East of Eden*. Among my grandfather's papers is an autographed copy of Steinbeck's acceptance speech for the Nobel Prize for Literature delivered in Stockholm, Sweden in December 1962.[20] Some of the correspondence between my grandfather and Steinbeck reveals the passion that the former continued to have relevant to national politics in the late 1950s and early 1960s. The letters sometimes reveal the scepticism with which he often viewed the national political scene, and the state of the country in general, proving the adage for subsequent generations that the "more things change, the more they remain the same." Extracts from the following letter from Hunter to Steinbeck is both perceptive and prescient, an indicator of future times on the American cultural landscape:

"Dear John—I have had for many years a contempt for Coronet magazine and its evil works but now I recant for a while because they published your beautiful letter which of course followed the good talk last fall at the moral place called Twenty One. Thank you and Stevenson and I hope it may encourage him to run. The blatant immorality of government, like Nixon;

---

[19] I do not know if my grandfather and his wife attended the Inauguration in January 1961. Unfortunately, on my part, this was one of the things I neglected to ask Edna Hunter Eller about before her death in 2004.

[20] Several first edition copies of Steinbeck's books, autographed to the Hunters by the author, were given to me by Edna M. Hunter Eller shortly before her death in 2004. These are now in possession of my daughter, Amanda Sullivan Wilson, who developed an appreciation for Steinbeck's prose while in high school literature studies.

of politics, like Chicago; of corporations, like television; is terribly obvious. The immorality of children, of teachers, of scientists, of ministers, is perfectly indicated in your letter. A far more sinister immorality is such as people—many people—even considering the election of a Nixon to the presidency—here is an immoral man in every conceivable definition—perhaps a presidential possibility...There is no point in attacking petty immorality or morality unless the BIG one is attacked—namely destroying forever Nixon and the profoundly evil forces behind him....We both are excited about your book—knowing nothing at all of its theme—This time send me an advance—or better, do what you did with Cannery Row and send a final galley proof for the collection. After you see Adlai you will have to let me know of his procedures at Los Angeles—I am not at all sure I get it. I think I would be OK with his accepting a big post in a Kennedy adm.—but only if he operated with complete loyalty to NNU...I think Eugene McCarthy's speech [at the 1960 Democratic National Convention] was one of the all-time greats—and completely off the cuff. Sorry you cannot be at the death watch on my 65th birthday—there will not be many more. But please be sure that you come see us on your way West (before or after the election?) There seems to be nothing very serious going on in the world. All leaders are going to campaign for a place at the public trough for three months and the President is having an extra month at golf and bridge and all's quiet over here. That, of course, is good. Even if the Congo and Cuba and Peking and a few others will not agree. I propose a ticket (if you can get a button) of Sam Snead for President and Charlie Goren for VP—if we have to have a golf-bridge playing pres..."[21]

----

[21] H.O. Hunter to John Steinbeck, undated, Howard O. Hunter papers, author's collection. My grandfather was notorious for not dating his letters. But the foregoing, which combines his thoughts from two of his letters with Steinbeck, was probably composed in the late summer of 1960, based on the political references contained in the communications. Adlai Stevenson had lost to Eisenhower in the elections of 1952 and 1956. Sam Snead was one of the world's leading professional golfers in the 1950s and Charles Goren was America's leading authority on contract bridge. Eisenhower was both an avid golfer and bridge player, before and during his presidency. Despite their differing political loyalties I believe my grandfather had great admiration for Eisenhower, who was certainly one of the greatest leaders in American military history. My grandfather's opinion about Richard M. Nixon speaks for itself. Of course, he did not live to see Nixon's election to two presidential terms in 1968 and 1972, followed by Nixon's Watergate scandal, and subsequent resignation from office, in 1973-74. In more recent political times, H.O. Hunter would clearly be regarded as a "centrist" Democrat, very much in the mode of President John F. Kennedy, rather than far left as the majority of Democrats are at the time of this writing.

Howard O. Hunter, photographed in 1963, the year before his death.

Additional gleanings from the Hunter papers are further indicative of the bond of friendship between Hunter, Steinbeck and Adlai E. Stevenson. Senator Stevenson was a prominent Illinois Democrat and had won the presidential nomination from his party in both the 1952 and 1956 elections, losing to Dwight D. Eisenhower on both occasions. During the Kennedy administration, Stevenson served as the U.S. Representative to the United Nations. In the summer of 1963, Stevenson wrote the following to Hunter:

"Dear Howard: John Steinbeck writes me that you have been ill. I am distressed to hear this, and I wish I were there and could call on such a great

45

and good and quiet man! The meeting of the NNU Club is long overdue and what better place than the bedside of its conspirator! But I shall have to content myself with hope for your recovery, and an early reunion. What with John's eye and your vocal chords—what an opportunity it would be for me! Cheers for a friend I seldom see! Yours, Adlai."[22]

As previously noted, Hunter retired in October 1963, after which he and his wife relocated from Chicago to Fort Lauderdale, Florida. Unfortunately, his retirement was very short-lived, for he died suddenly on February 22, 1964, at the age of sixty-eight. Hunter is buried in Baton Rouge, where also lie his parents.[23]

Howard O. Hunter was an exceedingly literate man, and an accomplished writer and historian in his own right. I recall occasions in my adolescence my grandfather sending me volumes on American maritime and naval history, books that I eagerly devoured and saved. These were the foundation for my growing interest for naval history that has endured all my life, perhaps now more so than ever. "HOH" clearly left many outstanding legacies to our contemporary family, as well as our descendants to follow.

* * *

Mary Jackson Hunter (1893-1968), my maternal grandmother, was the adopted (unsubstantiated) daughter of Dr. Henry Herbert Johnson (1861-1937) of Macon and his wife, Wilhelmina Wheeler Johnson (1872-1955). To date, I have not determined my grandmother Hunter's birth parents, likely from Tennessee. Herbert and Wilhelmina Johnson married in 1897. I warmly remember my great-grandmother Johnson, "Danum," from my earliest recollections of growing up at Cedar Point in the early-to-mid 1950s; she lived in

---

[22] Adlai E. Stevenson to H.O. Hunter, August 15, 1963, Howard O. Hunter papers. Despite my best efforts, I have been unable to ascertain just what the "NNU Club" was. Apparently, it is an "insiders" reference as it is mentioned jokingly several times in exchanges of letters between my grandfather, Steinbeck, and Stevenson.

[23] Some years later, Hunter's widow, Edna M. Hunter, remarried—an unfortunate marriage as she related to me many times. She lived in Spain for a time then, in 1973, returned to the United States where she resided, variously, in Atlanta, Fort Lauderdale, and Birmingham, Alabama, before returning to Fort Lauderdale where she died in March 2004. I was extremely close to Edna in the last thirty years of her life, as were my children, particularly Patrick and Amanda. Prior to her passing Edna Hunter Eller bequeathed to me for safekeeping all the remaining papers and photographs in her possession relating to Howard O. Hunter.

the "cottage" adjacent to the Johnsons' Cedar Point "big house" and many were the mornings I would indulge in a breakfast of hot tea and buttered toast with her as she regaled me with her stories of the past. Her husband, Dr. H.H. Johnson, a native of Houston County, Georgia, was another of those extraordinary individuals that have emerged among the forebears of my family. In Macon, he established a successful dental practice, being regarded as a pioneer in the advancement of twentieth century dental technology and served as president of the Georgia Dental Association. Macon also represents the genesis of our family's Cedar Point connection through Dr. Johnson's acquisition of property there in the early 1900s. Meanwhile, H.O. and Mary Hunter had two children, Howard Owen, Jr. (1922-1983) and my mother, Mary Kate (May 24, 1924-February 14, 1954). Both Owen and Mary Kate were born in Macon, Bibb County, Georgia, while their father was administering the southeastern Boy Scouts.

There is some uncertainty about my grandmother Hunter's early years. She was born January 8, 1893, in Tennessee. The Hunters' marriage certificate dated December 22, 1920, in Macon gives her middle name as Emily. However, 1900 census data 1900 validates her middle name as "Jane", and that she was born Jackson in Tennessee. The circumstances of her adoption by the Johnsons of Macon (or even if she actually *was* formally adopted), and precisely when, thus far remains unknown to me. As far as is known she never used "Johnson" as a surname before her marriage to Howard Hunter, and the "J" in her signed correspondence and was always understood to represent "Jackson" rather than "Jane" or "Johnson." She died at Quitman, Georgia, May 1, 1968 at the age of seventy-five and is buried in St. Andrew Cemetery, Darien, beside my mother and Wilhelmina Johnson.

The 1930 U.S. census reveals that Howard and Mary Hunter, with their two young children, Mary Kate and Owen, Jr., were living in Bridgeport, Connecticut, this being the period in which Hunter was a U.S. government civil servant in New England. The Hunters divorced in 1933; Mary and the two children relocated from Connecticut to McIntosh County where they resided in the Johnson house at Cedar Point. The 1940 McIntosh County census lists "Mary Jane Hunter" as a resident of Crescent (the post office for Cedar Point) with her two children, Howard Owen, Jr. and Mary Kate. Mary Jane Hunter is shown on this census as being the "head of household" at Cedar Point that also included her adoptive widowed mother, Wilhelmina Johnson.

Henry Herbert Johnson.

The family home at Cedar Point has an interesting history. The Johnsons were spending time at Cedar Point as early as 1901 based on the dates on faded photographs in my personal papers. The 1901 picture depicts a relatively young-looking Dr. Johnson displaying a pair of game birds after a hunt, with palm trees and the marsh in the background looking familiarly like the Cedar Point waterfront view. Another picture is dated May 13, 1925 and is inscribed "Dr. Johnson holding two 50-pound drum fish caught in Sapelo Sound." The marsh and creek in the background of this snapshot also appear to be that of Cedar Point. Also among my personal papers is the documentation by which our family's property at Cedar Point was acquired. A letter dated November 19, 1911 written by C.M. Atwood of Valona to Dr. Johnson states, in part: "Enclosed find plat of my lot at Cedar Point, price $1,000.00. Papa has never made deed to me but he was willing for me to sell. Would like to sell by January 1st and I will appreciate your efforts in helping me make this sale & would like to have some of your friends on the place. Papa expects to be at Cedar Point while you are there." The survey plat accompanying this note, pictured on the next page of this book, delineates with clarity the property overlooking Cedar Creek upon which Dr. Johnson subsequently built the family home, the "big house," several years

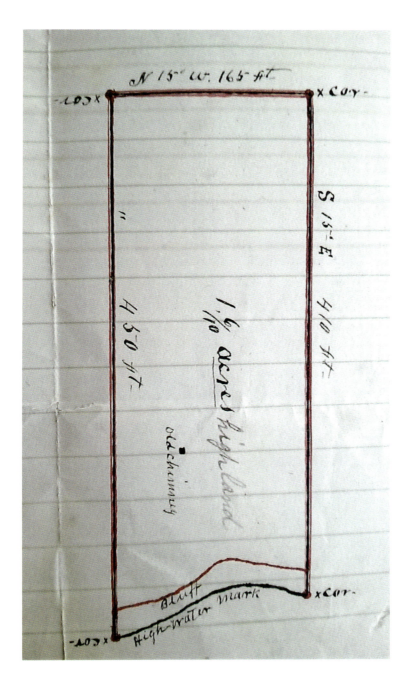

1911 plat of Cedar Point waterfront lot bought by Dr. H.H. Johnson on which he built his home overlooking Cedar Creek. It was later split into two lots. My 2018 house was built 15 feet to the right of the spot marked "old chimney."

later. The plat depicts a 1.6-acre tract, later divided by Dr. Johnson into separate lots for family members. The plat is meticulously drawn in red and black ink on a yellowing, legal size sheet of paper. The original 1911 (which survives and is among my personal papers) plat depicting the longitudinal Johnson lot fronting on Cedar Creek and the marsh is displayed on a wall in my home built on the same lot in 2018—tangible testimony that I have come full circle, three-sixty, the beginning to end of my life on the McIntosh tidewater. On the sketch there is marked an "old chimney" (see drawing) precisely on what was later the property line when Dr. Johnson divided his property, with the adjoining lot going to the possession of his wife, then a son, Wheeler Johnson.[24] I have been intrigued as to the provenance of this chimney. As it appears on the 1911 plat, it obviously marks the spot where a structure on the site stood much earlier, presumably in the 1800s. Could it have been the home of one of the Atwood family members, who for generations had owned most of the Cedar Point tract? Perhaps it was that of George Elliott Atwood (1849-1914), one of the sons of Henry S. and Ann Margaret McIntosh Atwood whose cotton plantation was at Cedar Point until the time of the Civil War. Or possibly John McIntosh Atwood (1849-1933), the twin brother of George. It's an interesting possibility, because one of the children of John M. McIntosh and Clara LaRoche Atwood, Elizabeth King "Lizzie," died at the age of three in 1882 and is buried in the little cemetery just a few yards from my Cedar Point house, a plot that overlooks the marshes toward Crescent and Baisden's Bluff. Another child in the same plot, John Cabaness Atwood, died at the age of two years and seven months in 1883, the child of George and Sophie LaRoche Atwood.[25]

---

[24] Two additional similar-sized longitudinal lots adjoining the original 1911 acquisition were later bought by Dr. Johnson, one of which went to my grandmother, Mary J. Hunter, upon which, in 1956, she built a new house. The four family lots all passed to other entities from 1969 on, until my fortuitous acquisition of the original "big house" lot in 2017, thus returning a piece of Cedar Point back into our family. Interestingly, I acquired the property from a descendant of Addie Atwood Hubbard. She and her husband were close Cedar Point friends of my parents. William "Bill" Hubbard was one of my father's partners in the Cedar Point seafood venture following World War II.

[25] An older brother of George E. and John M. Atwood, William Henry Atwood (1836-1912), was one of McIntosh County's most prominent citizens in the postbellum era. About 1890, he and his wife, Tallulah Butts Atwood (1850-1909), built the two-story Cedar Point house (still standing in

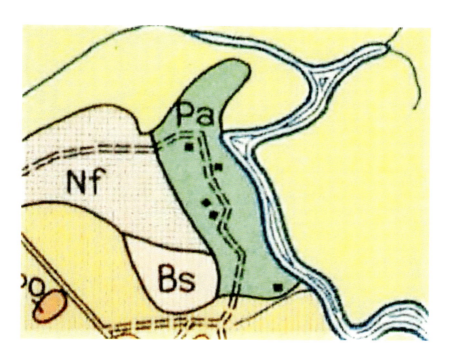

Cedar Point from a 1929 soil map, showing the location of H.H. Johnson's house, the topmost square.

Whatever the case, the "old chimney" has long since disappeared, but was once situated no more than fifteen feet from the south side of where my house now sits—which itself is precisely upon the spot where Dr. Johnson built his house almost a century before I built mine. Dr. Johnson built the two-story white frame house on his Cedar Point tract about 1923, the property being shaded by live oaks and palms, with a southeast exposure over the marsh toward

---

2024) overlooking Cedar Creek less than a hundred yards south of the lots H.H. Johnson acquired a few years later. The Atwoods' son, Henry Grantland Atwood (1872-1942) inherited the house, living there until his death during World War II. His widow Jane Woodward Atwood (1897-1998) lived in half of the house for many years afterwards, certainly through my childhood and adolescence at Cedar Point. Adeline "Addie" Atwood Hubbard (1908-2008) of Atlanta, who owned the other half of the house and lived there part-time, was a friend of my parents, and whose descendant sold me the Cedar Point lot originally bought by my great-grandfather Johnson in 1911. Addie Hubbard's husband was William D. "Bill" Hubbard (1912-1988) who ran the Cedar Point cannery with my father and uncle for several years after the Second World War.

The marsh, creek and the "Point" at Cedar Point from the waterfront at our home, a lifelong familiar view.

Creighton and the inland waterway, ideally situated for the cooling southeast breezes in summer, while affording a modicum of buffer from northeasters in fall and winter. Dr. Johnson died at Cedar Point at the age of seventy-five on May 23, 1937, the same year as my other maternal great-grandfather, Dr. T.M. Hunter. Dr. Johnson is buried in Macon.

The family's Cedar Point connection was thus made, and the

H.H. Johnson house (center) at Cedar Point, 1940s. Johnson cottage is at left, later occupied by his widow.

scene of my childhood and adolescence was secured. Parenthetically, the Cedar Point house accidentally burned in 1980. My grandmother, Mary J. Hunter, had in 1956 built a separate home overlooking Cedar Creek for herself two lots south of the "big house," a stone's throw from the abandoned oyster cannery. My own home, built in 2018 on the ancestral Cedar Point property, is sited precisely on the footprint of the two-story wood-frame residence built by my great-grandfather Johnson in the early 20s.

In south Georgia, my father attended grammar school in the small town of Ashburn, then later attended high school in nearby Tifton (class of 1939) where he excelled academically, and as an athlete, earning all-star honors on the football and baseball teams. His father, my paternal grandfather, Roy Sullivan, later had a successful insurance career, working many years from an office at the Bowen-Donaldson Funeral Home on Love Avenue in Tifton, an imposing two-story early 1900s brick edifice still very familiar to me in my mind's eye. I have pleasant memories of summer afternoons in the 1950s and 1960s accompanying my grandfather on his insurance debit route along the dusty back roads of Tift County, calling on locals at their farmhouses, and even occasionally in the midst of their tobacco or peanut fields. I recall with fondness those simple south Georgia days, going back and forth from the coast to Tifton in the summers. A highlight of those pleasant days in Tifton was the noon meal, a repast always referred to as dinner—never as "lunch" in that

My grandfather Roy Sullivan and myself, ca. 1964. I was about 17.

south Georgia culture, with supper—not "dinner"—served in the early evening (often consisting of dinner leftovers). Meals were prepared daily from scratch by my grandmother, Willie Lemon Sullivan. She was the finest cook, clearly an inherited skill, and she always featured traditional home-cooked menus comprised of fried chicken or pork chops, with pot roast on Sundays, field peas and snap beans, butter beans, mashed potatoes, fried corn, sliced tomatoes, and homemade biscuits, all washed down with copious quantities of sweet iced tea. After supper, there would often be a watermelon cut shared with the neighbors in the backyard while waiting for the minor league baseball game to begin at nearby Eve Park, which we watched from the yard.

In 1941, my father was attending the University of Georgia when America entered the Second World War late in the year. Like so many of his contemporaries, he immediately joined the ranks of the military as forces were being mobilized across the country. As a lieutenant in the infantry and army airborne corps, my father served with distinction in the campaigns for North Africa in 1942-43, and later in Sicily and Italy where he fought in some of the most difficult battles of the European theater, being awarded the Bronze Star for valor in action and the Purple Heart for being wounded in battle

My mother, Mary Kate Hunter, as a teenage girl. Photographed on the front lawn of the Cedar Point "big house," about 1938 or 1939.

(L-r) my mother, Mary Kate Hunter, Wanda Atwood and my mother's brother, H. Owen Hunter, Jr., ca. 1943.

against German forces. In early 1944, he was in the midst of the fighting against Axis forces in the battles around Monte Cassino, one of the most intensely fought and costly ground actions of the war, and an outcome that eventually opened the Allies' path toward the liberation and occupation of Rome.

Prior to the war my father and mother met during one of the former's visits to the Georgia coast from Tifton, or perhaps Athens.

My father Roy Earl Sullivan with his wife-to-be and my mom, Mary Kate Hunter, 1944.

My parents at Cedar Point, about 1948. I'm at the
bottom, obviously with little interest in posing for the camera.

My mother of course had grown up at Cedar Point and graduated
from Darien High School in 1940 at the age of sixteen. The photo of
Mary Kate on page 55 is one of my favorites—the All-American
coastal Georgia girl! As did her mother before her, my mother chose
nursing as a career, and pursued her studies in medicine at Valdosta
State College before and during World War II.

In 1945 my parents, Roy Earl Sullivan and Mary Kate Hunter,
were married in Atlanta and then moved to my mother's home at
Cedar Point. Following their service in the recent war, my father,
with my uncle, H.O. Hunter, Jr., and their friend William Hubbard,
leased from Mrs. Jane Atwood the oyster cannery at Cedar Point, a
few hundred feet from our home place. The cannery had been begun
much earlier by Mrs. Atwood's late husband, Henry G. Atwood (d.
1942). She wished to keep the operation open, thus the partnership
of the three war vets came along at a propitious time for all parties.
The Cedar Point Canning Company was under lease to the three
young men who, like thousands of others in coastal Georgia during
the period, were returning home from military service seeking work.

Oyster factory at Cedar Point, ca. 1930s, only a few yards from our family property and my present home. (Author's collection)

Good jobs were at a premium, and the potential profits in oysters seemed a good prospect at the time. Sullivan, Hunter and Hubbard managed the Cedar Point factory, shipping processed oysters to the Campbell Company in Atlanta, as well as selling oysters by the gallon to local and area distributors. Owen Hunter had a shrimp boat, the *White Rose*, supplementing the operation. There was also an oyster bateau towboat, the *Roma*. The *Roma* was a workboat that towed the oyster bateaux to the oyster beds and back to the factory. Sometime in the early 1950s, the old boat was towed around to the back side of Cedar Point and abandoned in the high marsh near the tree fringe. The author recalls seeing it rotting away there in his adolescent years. Nothing remains of the vessel. The *White Rose* shrimp boat was operated by the author's uncle, Howard O. Hunter, Jr. out of Cedar Point. According to my father, Roy Earl Sullivan, who spent many a day working on the boat with my Uncle Hunter, the *White Rose* developed mechanical trouble and sank while under tow one day in Sapelo Sound. The vessel was unsalvageable. I have often wondered in what part of the Sound the *White Rose* foundered in. In those days the great majority of shrimp boats trawled in the sounds, being too fragile to fish "outside" the barrier islands except in optimal weather conditions. Based on my historical research over the years, the *White Rose* was only one of many vessels documented to have sunk in the

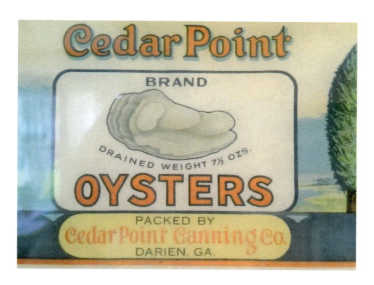

Canning label, 1940s, from the Cedar Point oyster factory adjacent to our home. (Author's collection)

Sound over 150-plus years, mostly due to adverse weather, and often challenging surface conditions in the Sound.

The partners ended activity at Cedar Point in 1949, but it continued to operate on an irregular basis under lease from Jane Atwood into the mid-1950s. The Ploeger cannery at Darien was the last such facility to operate on a large scale in McIntosh County; it suspended operations about 1960 due to declining harvests and reduced habitat. As for the Cedar Point factory, it gradually fell into ruins. In my childhood, I recall playing amid the abandoned factory with its rusting tin roof, and inside, an artesian well continually flowed fresh water through a lead pipe; shell banks lined the creek bank a short distance away, the shells blanched by years of sun exposure. Eventually, the facility disappeared, its lumber sold for scrap, and the property sold by Jane Atwood. In the mid-1980s, an attractive private residence was constructed on the foundations of the factory by Rundle and Jeannine Cook, they being newcomers to McIntosh County.

Meanwhile, the legacy of the *White Rose* lives on, both in the handsome carved model shown on page 61, and in that I named my new home at Cedar Point "White Rose Cottage" at the suggestion of my friend Jim Klippel (see the photo on page 2 of this book) who produced the model, and also designed my home. It is my tribute to my family's Cedar Point legacy and its post-World War II commercial fishing activities just a few feet away. Occasionally I walk next door to

The White Rose *at Cedar Point oyster factory dock, ca. 1947 or 48.*

my grandmother Hunter's former property and savor the view, the memories, and the tangible vestiges of my adolescence in the 1950s and 1960s on and around that waterfront (see the image on page 48 for the modern-day perspective that I had as a kid growing up–little has changed). The old cannery is long gone but the concrete foundations remain; the rotting pilings of the docks are still there too, and a pile of oyster shells repose amid the nearby marsh, with distant vistas of the inland waterway, Creighton and Sapelo beyond, just as F.R. Goulding described it on page 14 of this account.

As a toddler of only three or four, I have only vague memories of the post-war Cedar Point activity. Family photo albums depict many black and white images of my father and mother in various activities at Cedar Point and enjoying social activities at St. Simons Island with their South Georgia friends. There is one photo favorite of mine–it is of my mother pushing me in a stroller along the little sidewalk linking the four family properties. Mary Kate is looking back at the photographer–presumably my father–as she proceeds along. I distinctly recall that the late 1940s and early 1950s were happy times

Model of the White Rose *by Jim Klippel, based on the photo on p. 60.*

for our family at Cedar Point. There were many gatherings of friends, boat outings, oyster roasts, trips to the beach, Christmas at the "big house" and overwhelming amounts of food, drink and illuminating conversation. There was also lots of time spent with my first cousin, H.O. "Woody" Hunter, III, son of Owen and Wanda Atwood Hunter. Woody and I are the same age, we being born in the immediate aftermath of the Second World War—early "Baby Boomers." On reflection, there was no better time and place in which to live. We were the lucky ones, born as the sons and daughters of the Greatest Generation" that had lived and survived a depression and two major wars. No wonder that wherever I went later in life, I always came home to "smell the marshes," and savor the memories of times past and the people I shared them with.

In 1949, my father gave up the seafood business and re-entered the U.S. Army as an officer, determining to make the military his career. He subsequently served with distinction in the Korean Conflict, 1950-52. I have memories as a child of five travelling across the Pacific Ocean on a military transport ship from Seattle, Washington to Yokohama, Japan with my mother, and other families in similar circumstances, to join my father during his overseas duty.

Mary Kate Hunter Sullivan, with the author, about 1950.

While my father was in Korea, my mother and I lived for a year or more in a two-level apartment at Sendai, Japan, and I had two delightful Japanese nursemaids *(amahs)*. My father was subsequently posted to Fort Benning, Georgia in 1952. During this time, in my seventh year, I became acutely aware of the frequent, and increasingly debilitating, illnesses of my mother. Our family trips from Columbus to the coast at Cedar Point became less frequent as my mother's health declined. It was a terribly low period in my life, becoming the saddest I had ever experienced when my mother succumbed to pancreatic cancer on Valentine's Day, 1954 at Walter Reed Hospital in Washington, D.C. with my father by her side, and myself with my grandmother Hunter at Cedar Point getting the awful news via a long-distance telephone call. Mary Kate Sullivan was only twenty-nine years old with a whole lifetime ahead of her. My mother left me with both warm memories and her coastal Georgia roots. For each of those I have been forever grateful over the succeeding years, never forgetting where I came from, and what I achieved later in my literary life through her coastal legacies.

Following the death of my mother on February 14, 1954 from cancer at the age of twenty-nine (an occurrence, not surprisingly, traumatizing to me at the age of seven), my adolescent years in the 1950s and 1960s in McIntosh County are a tapestry of memories, of

Myself, my mother, Mary Kate Hunter Sullivan, and an unidentified friend, about 1951, in Japan during my father's Korean War service.

an uncomplicated life where the biggest daily decisions usually revolved around what creek or ballast island we were going to explore in our plywood boat powered by a little 3-horsepower outboard engine. The grownups were reading the *Darien News* and discussing things that were foreign to us uncomprehending kids—U.S. 17, the main north-south conveyor through the county on which Florida-bound tourists (Yankees) were allegedly being surreptitiously hustled at roadside gambling houses, and how the talk of a proposed new "super-highway" called the Interstate was going to undo all the alleged illegitimacy. There was Sunday school and church at Darien Presbyterian, a weekly ritual, and lasting bonds of friendship established; Saturday matinees at the Darien Theater where one could gain admittance, a Coke and a bag of popcorn all for a quarter in those days. At Stebbins Grocery & Hardware next door to the theater, Bama (as I called my grandmother Hunter) had a charge account, the perfect setup for a grandson who regularly frequented the old store for candy, chips and other treats, with friendly conversation with Jimmy and Frieda Stebbins, whose tolerance and patience with me amazes me as I write this; occasional stops at Williams Brothers grocery store and hardware at Meridian where Frank and Will Williams held court; and the pleasing aroma from drying deer tongue leaves at nearby Hudson community remains indelibly imprinted upon my memory; childhood crushes at Darien public school; rambling around the shrimp docks under the watchful eye of tolerant fishermen on the Darien waterfront, at Cedar Point, Valona and Hudson Creek; fountain cherry cokes at Rogers' Rexall Drugs in town; the Rabb family and the Darien Dry Cleaners; building huts of scrap lumber and roofing tin on a dredge spoil hammock on the inland waterway near Creighton; and then there was the day some of us boys skipped school for a couple of hours one day in 1960 to walk to the county courthouse, slip in through the back entrance and hear the testimony of Mrs. Reynolds in the divorce trial with her husband R.J. Reynolds, owner of Sapelo Island. At the time, that was about the biggest news that had hit our parts in ages. Memories...

Food was always in such abundance. Fresh garden vegetables grown on the premises; fresh eggs from the chicken coop out back of the big house—as a child I cried for hours the first time I witnessed my father or my grandmother chop the head off a hen, after which it as plucked and prepared for fresh fried chicken. Bama always told me not to worry, the hen never felt a thing when the axe came down on its neck. I wasn't sure I believed her in my childhood innocence!

In the coastal low country rice, prepared in a variety of ways, was Always traditional staple. Rice in some form was an essential part of the diet of the coastal South from Charleston to Savannah to New Orleans, and my grandmother Mary Hunter (Bama) always had rice at least one meal a day, whether steamed to be topped with gravy, or my favorite, rice topped with shrimp, spices and tomato sauce—

I'm on familiar waters: Boating on Shellbluff Creek, Valona, 1980, age 34.

shrimp creole, another traditional low country recipe. Naturally, where we were at Cedar Point, and the coast in general, seafood was in abundance—shrimp caught with a cast net in front of our house, or crabs gathered in the nearby creek at low tide with chicken necks and dip net. Like the doomed chicken mentioned above, I always felt sadness when Bama, wielding her tongs, put the live crabs, one by one, into a boiling pot of water—as before "they didn't feel a thing!" Nonetheless, as my forebears always said, one could never go hungry on the coast with all its natural bounty.

In the spring of 1955 (in my third grade year at the Darien school) during his continued posting at Fort Benning, my father married Alcye Lois Streetman of Columbus who over the years became my friend and mentor, an amazing woman in her own right, and with whom I grew increasingly close with the passage of time, even more so in recent years with our shared interest in Southern history, family genealogy, and our shared and enjoyable experiences with the Streetman and allied families of Columbus over the years. From the summer of 1955 until the spring of 1957, my father, Alcye and I lived in Hawaii, on the island of Oahu where he was stationed at Schofield Barracks as a company commander. The first year we lived in a beach house on the north side of Oahu, at Mokuleia (we went swimming in the ocean on Christmas Day), where I attended the fourth grade at the nearby Waialua elementary school. The second year we lived on post at Schofield and I attended fifth grade at the public school near Wahiawa, where most of the children of military and naval personnel attended. I have vivid memories of school field trips to the Pearl Harbor navy base—this was a mere fifteen years after the Japanese sneak attack—and other sites in and around Honolulu learning about Hawaiian history and culture—orchids, hibiscus, poi, pineapple, lots of alohas, and a delicious native sweet candy whose name escapes me, but with the consistency of taffy. My first experience on an airplane, at the age of ten, was on the return to the United States in 1956, Honolulu to San Francisco, where we spent several days.

It was in the seventh grade at the Darien public school, 1958-59, that I acquired my first sense of, and appeal for, the history of our county, our coast and the state of Georgia; it was then also that Bessie Mary Lewis began to define my future relevance as a historian of McIntosh County and coastal Georgia. It may be stated without the slightest equivocation that had there been no Bessie Lewis, there would have been no yours truly as a historian—at least in a role as a researcher and author of the history of the low country region that Bessie Lewis loved and described so well. I first knew "Miss Bessie" as a child growing up in the county. My earliest recollection of this remarkable woman was watching—and listening—with fascination as she skillfully played the organ during Sunday services at the Darien Presbyterian Church. Later, I became aware of her role as the county historian. In my adolescence I was already developing an interest in local history, and Miss Bessie took me under her wing on a number of occasions to nurture that interest. I believe she took me on as a "special project" in those innocent years of the late 1950s and early 1960s because her influence became the motivating factor in providing a path to my own research and writing of local history years later. Miss Bessie's mentorship and influence remains with me even now as I write these words in my memoir.

Lewis spent time with me relating stories of the history of the area. As an impressionable twelve-year old taking seventh-grade classes in Georgia history in 1958, I accompanied her on some of her "rambles" about the county. She had coordinated the placement of thirty state historical markers in various locales for which she had written the texts, from the South Newport River to Butler's Island, and all the key places in between. All of her markers are still in place and have been read by thousands of residents and visitors to the county.

The view from home after a summer thunderstorm: An early evening sun reflects over the marsh and creek.

Parenthetically, I have carried on the Lewis tradition regarding state markers, as I have researched and written the texts for half a dozen markers in McIntosh County, and fifteen markers in Bryan County on behalf of the Lower Altamaha and Richmond Hill historical societies, respectively.

Attending public school in Darien in the first through third grades, and sixth through eighth, amplified my initial interest in local history, and my early mentors in that regard were memorable. My junior high school teachers at the Darien school, Anne Whorton and Rena Thomson, both encouraged my interest in Georgia and coastal history. Numerous class field trips over several years to Fort King George, including walking down the sandy road from the schoolhouse to the site at Lower Bluff, when there was no fort left, no museum, no reconstructed blockhouse, only a marker and a burial ground, whetted my appetite for local history. I recall Bessie Lewis sharing with me her opinion that Viking explorers from Iceland may actually have set foot in what became McIntosh County half a millennium before Columbus came to America. "I think the Vikings may have attempted to settle on Creighton Island," she once told me. I looked up from where we sat on the front porch of our

The view from the front porch near sundown, 2020.

house at Cedar Point and viewed in the near distance the outline of Creighton just across the marshes. Perhaps that was the moment that I became "hooked on history." I realized then how interesting and diverse was the history of our part of the coast. That was likely—subconsciously, if not in reality—the point at which I determined to pursue my own investigations, perhaps even follow in the footsteps of Lewis—as if anyone could actually fill her shoes! Miss Bessie died in 1983 at the age of ninety-four and I never had the opportunity to properly recognize in a public way while she lived the positive impact she had on my career. My 2016 biography of Lewis, *A Low Country Diary*, with my commentary on her wonderful writings, was my lasting and permanent tribute to her.[26]

I attended Columbus High School, and there that I acquired an interest in high school and college athletics, an enthusiasm that led to the publication of my first book at the age of thirty in 1976.[27]

---

[26] Buddy Sullivan, *Low Country Diary: Bessie Mary Lewis and McIntosh County, Georgia* (Lower Altamaha Historical Society, Darien, 2016). The majority of this book is a selection of my favorite Lewis columns about history and animals extracted from her weekly column, "Low Country Diary."

[27] *Dress Her in Orange and Blue, The Story of Columbus High, the Bi-City and Georgia Prep Sports.* The book covers high school athletics in Columbus and

68

Following graduation from LaGrange College in 1968 with a degree in history, I served six months as sports editor of the *LaGrange Daily News*—I was then supposedly the youngest sports editor of a daily newspaper in the state.

Nineteen sixty-eight was a momentous year for impressionable 21-year-old baby boomers. Against the often drug-fueled backdrop of the Beatles, the Rolling Stones, Simon & Garfunkel, and the Righteous Brothers, there was the dissent and frustration of an incomprehensible Vietnam War, and the relentless student protests against the war, burning draft cards, and President Johnson's famous "I shall not run" for re-election televised speech because of the vicissitudes of that conflict. There were two horrific assassinations within months of each other—Senator Robert Kennedy, in California on the way to a probable victory in that year's presidential election, and Martin Luther King one terrible spring evening in Memphis.

These events resurrected the traumatic, emotional recollections of the assassination of President Kennedy five years earlier on November 22nd, 1963, news I first heard in sixth period study hall at Columbus High. We were getting ready to depart for an out-of-town state playoff football game (we were No. 2 in the state at the time). It was a terrible afternoon and night—it was the signature moment of our generation, just as the terrorist attacks of 9-11 would be for my children thirty-eight years later. We cancelled our trip, the football game was played anyway, and we lost the game on the day JFK died, our eyes glued to the black-and-images unfolding from Dallas as the news flashes from Walter Cronkite rolled endlessly on.

The 1968 national election season was marked by riots and protests, concluding with the ascendancy of Richard Nixon to the presidency. Then finally, mercifully, that fateful year ended when, on Christmas Eve, three American astronauts orbiting the moon, the first human beings to do so, took turns reading from the Book of Genesis with the incredibly beautiful bluish hues of the distant planet Earth gleaming in the background through the window of Apollo Eight. Their names were Borman, Lovell and Anders, and watching that achievement in real time, in color, on television seemed to me the most amazing thing that had ever happened—more meaningful even than the actual first moon landing that came seven months later by Armstrong and Aldrin. After experiencing the

---

among the larger schools of Georgia from 1908 to 1976. Looking back on the volume now, I almost cringe at the sophomoric inelegance of my writing in those days. I had a lot to learn.

Thunderheads at sunset over the Cedar Point marshes.

Kennedy assassination as a high school senior, and the turbulence of the Sixties that followed, the Christmas Eve moon orbits seemed to restore some sanity and peace to a chaotic world, even if only for a few peaceful hours. And I realized then how proud I was to be an American...

This being the height of the Vietnam War, I received the inevitable draft notice, followed by eight weeks of infantry basic training at nearby Fort Benning, then two years of active duty at Fort Belvoir, Virginia outside Washington, D.C., largely in administrative assignments. While in the Army, I was enabled to continue my sports writing with part-time employment covering high school sports in Alexandria and Arlington, Virginia, after which I returned (following a two-month stop for a cup of coffee with a daily in Petersburg, Virginia) to Columbus as the high school sports editor for the *Columbus Enquirer*. There, I covered high school and college football games and learned a great deal about the newspaper business. Throughout the 1970s and 1980s, I worked at several daily papers—high school sports coverage in Columbus, followed by a stint as a college football writer at the *Florida Times-Union* in Jacksonville, Florida in 1973. Then came a return to LaGrange as sports editor of the *LaGrange Daily News*, where I renewed many old acquaintances and made as many new ones in a rewarding, happy eight years. This was followed by three years, from 1982 to 1985, covering college football and professional golf at the *Savannah Morning News*.

From 1968 to 1985, my primary, and preferred, sports reporting "beat" was always high school and college football, and more specifically, football at the University of Georgia. It was in this capacity that I established a lasting friendship with Vince Dooley, coach and athletic director of the Georgia Bulldogs for forty years; also, Coach Erskine Russell (before he went to Georgia Southern in 1981) and others on the coaching staff, as well as Dan Magill, Claude Felton and Greg McGarity in the UGA sports information office, the latter becoming athletic director at UGA years later. I covered all manner of college games from Southeastern Conference headliners to bowl games to national championships, at my sports writing jobs in Columbus, LaGrange, Jacksonville and Savannah. I regularly reported on Georgia, and occasionally Georgia Tech, Auburn and Alabama, the latter during the years of the great Coach Bear Bryant.[28]

At LaGrange, near the Alabama state line, I often travelled to Auburn where I became close to the sports information staff and knew Coach Shug Jordan, one of the outstanding gentlemen of Southern football. At Georgia games in Athens and elsewhere from 1968 to 1985, I had the pleasure of being a regular in the press box with the luminaries of the sports writing profession—Furman Bisher and Jesse Outlar of the *Atlanta Journal-Constitution,* and Harley Bowers of the *Macon Telegraph,* among others. I was in Atlanta Stadium the spring night in 1974 when the Braves' Henry Aaron hit his 715th career home run to break Babe Ruth's record; and covered professional tennis and golf regularly, including a memorable six days in Augusta covering the 1985 Masters (won by Bernhard Langer). I knew and interviewed Chris Evert long before she became an

---

[28] Buddy Sullivan Papers, Collection 2433, Georgia Historical Society, contains original copies of correspondence relating to my coverage of sports from 1968 to 1985. My friendship with Vince Dooley evolved to a new collegiality between us with our common interests in the research and writing of history. Dooley, who died in 2022, was a prolific author, and an exceptionally gifted historian; his later research led him to undertake studies of aspects of coastal Georgia history, a subject in which we shared information. He was far more than a gifted football coach.

Vince Dooley spent a day with me on Sapelo in November 2008. Here we are after arriving on the ferry.

international tennis star, and rubbed elbows with some of the best-known coaches and athletes of the 70s and 80s.

Covering Georgia in 1980 with *LaGrange Daily News* was the highlight of my years as a sports writer. The most electrifying moment of that season, perhaps in all of Bulldog sports history, occurred not in New Orleans when the national championship was won by Georgia, but in Jacksonville at the annual Cocktail Party against Florida. I was standing on the Georgia sidelines with other writers very late in the game, the undefeated and No. 2-ranked Bulldogs behind, and thinking all was lost, when Lindsay Scott ran right past me, so close I could have reached out and grabbed his arm as he went by, racing to the far end zone to culminate a 93-yard pass play from Belue with a minute left, the roars of 80,000-plus people almost deafening, a miracle fourth-down play that overcame Florida, 26-21, and served as the springboard to the national title. I still have a faded portion of the front page of the Jacksonville *Florida Times Union* that displays a seven-column wide color photo above the fold showing Scott's run to glory—and there I am right there in the middle of the photo frantically urging Scott on as he races past me (*Run Lindsay! Run Lindsay!* in the immortal words of the late UGA announcer Larry Munson that day). A moment frozen forever in time for Georgia, for my friend Vince Dooley, and for me personally.

It was a splendid and exciting time in my professional life, by all accounts. Experiencing the 1980 championship season first-hand resulted in my second published book, issued in 1981, *Hunker Down! The Story of Dooley's 'Dogs.*[26] I covered an amazing four-year run for Georgia, and Dooley—12-0, 10-2, 11-1, and 10-1-1 records from 1980 through '83. I accompanied the team to bowl games all four years, the first three to the Sugar Bowl, the reward for three consecutive SEC championships, and the fourth to Dallas to witness a stunning upset of heavily favored Texas in the Cotton Bowl. Added to the mix was Walker's Heisman Trophy award in 1982, the season the unbeaten, top-ranked Bulldogs lost a close game to Penn State for the national championship in New Orleans. Had that game gone the other way (and it very easily could, and should, have) it would have been two national titles in three years for Georgia.

In the mid-eighties, I laid my professional sports writing career to rest, putting the cover on my old Smith-Corona portable typewriter for the last time at the Masters in Augusta in the spring of 1985, my last important sports writing assignment of a career that had begun seventeen years earlier. The machine had seen the front row perches of many a press box all over the southeast, from New Orleans to Knoxville, from Auburn, Tuscaloosa, Birmingham, and Atlanta to Jacksonville, Dallas, Athens, Gainesville, and Jackson, Mississippi—with so many frenzied days and nights of writing football stories in the press box under the pressure of newspaper deadlines in those simpler days of filing our pieces over the telephone, or via Western Union (these were the 70s and 80s, before the advent of portable computers and laptops, or even before devices known as telecopiers or fax machines had made their appearance).

I continued to cover Georgia during my three years at the *Savannah Morning News* from 1982 to 1985, a move largely made possible by my friend and fellow writer Frank Tilton. I followed the team to three straight Southeastern Conference championships and trips to major bowls four years in a row—three Sugar Bowls in New Orleans and the Cotton Bowl in Dallas.[29] Vince Dooley, the dean of SEC coaches in 2022, won 201 games in 25 years.

---

[29] Out of these experiences emerged my monograph, *Hunker Down! The Story of Dooley's 'Dogs* (1981), covering the Dooley coaching era from 1964-81. My friend Frank Tilton, a native Savannahian, has lived in McIntosh County for many years, at Fairhope. We have been friends since the 70s. Long-retired Coach Dooley, along with "Tillie," myself and countless thousands of other Georgia Bulldog fans, waited—and waited—for another national

In the summer of 1985, after seventeen years covering sports for several daily newspapers in Georgia and Florida, I returned to my McIntosh County roots, to Darien, where I served a productive and gratifying eight years as editor of the weekly *Darien News* under the tutelage of two more friends and mentors, Charles and Maude Williamson, owners and publishers of the paper. It was early in my work at the *News* that I began, almost by accident, my first serious investigations into local and coastal history, work that went hand-in-hand with the writing and organizational skills honed by seventeen years in the newspaper business to that point. A catalyst was the observance in 1986 of the 250th anniversary of the founding of Darien.

During this time, I was aware that Darien and McIntosh County had never had a comprehensive book written about its history, and that despite a number of short studies written over the years by Bessie Lewis, nothing of substance had been produced. An in-depth history of the county remained to be written. With the encouragement of many in the community, including those in the Lower Altamaha Historical Society, I made the commitment to research and write the county history, and publish the book that Lewis always intended to prepare herself, but was never able to do before her death in 1983. Thus, the first edition of *Early Days on the Georgia Tidewater* appeared in late 1990, with five subsequent printings to 2001, and later, my revision, expansion and updating of the volume in a softcover edition in 2018. My last encounter with Lewis had occurred in the summer of 1979, a visit to her home at Pine Harbor where her library was brimming with books, manuscripts and research documents—a veritable gold mine of the bits, pieces, memorabilia, and ephemera of coastal Georgia history. By then in my thirties, I was, perhaps for the first time, able to sit and converse intelligently with this doyenne of local historical matters—a long way removed from the wide-eyed lad who years earlier had so much to learn from her. I told Bessie that day that all these collections of material were the basis for which a multi-volume

---

football championship for forty-one years after the glory of 1980 before finally being rewarded with another title. Georgia defeated defending champion Alabama 33-18 to cap a 14-1 season in 2021. Coach Dooley passed away at the age of 90 in October 2022. Three months later Georgia made it back-to-back titles, beating TCU 65-7 to finish a perfect 15-0.

Thunderheads over Doboy Sound and the open sea beyond.

work of local history could be prepared, and that she needed to write it, even though she was ninety years of age at the time—but what an energetic ninety-year-old she was! Bessie replied that that was indeed her intention, to finally prepare a comprehensive history of the county. Unfortunately, her declining health would not permit her to write the in-depth book she wanted, perhaps the only real goal that eluded her during a lifetime devoted to compiling the history of the region. When she died four years after our last meeting, I resolved one day to try to write the book that she was never able to do herself. The result was the first edition of *Early Days on the Georgia Tidewater*, published seven years later, in 1990. It is a book heavily influenced by the research of Lewis, a book that has as its underlying theme the devotion to McIntosh County's past that she had inspired in me over the years. I hope she would have approved of this fruit of my own labors, for in many ways, *Early Days* is every bit as much hers as it is mine.

During my eight years of editing the *Darien News,* and the following twenty years as the manager of the Sapelo Island National Estuarine Research Reserve, and in the ten years since departing Sapelo, I have been able to produce a number of publications on coastal history. These ranged from two edited journals of rice planters (antebellum Roswell King, Jr. and postbellum John G. Legare), an examination of Darien's post-Civil War timber industry, including the editing of the Thomas Hilton memoirs, a comprehensive history of Bryan County, similar in style, research and depth to the McIntosh County history, and in 2003, a 200-plus page review of the history of Georgia as a volunteer project for the Georgia Historical Society, *Georgia: A State History, 1733-2000.* All of my publications will be found in the bibliography in this book.

I cannot say that all this historical work came about on my own independent initiative. I could not have gone nearly as far in my research without the friendship and professional collegiality of other special people that I have encountered along my path. Bessie Lewis was only the first. The late Malcolm Bell of Savannah, whose 1987 book on the Butlers and Frances Anne Kemble will long stand as the definitive account, was encouraging of all my work on McIntosh County; Kenneth H. Thomas, state historian for the Department of Natural Resources, and my contemporary (we graduated from the same class at Columbus High School) was immeasurably helpful with my Sapelo research in the 1990s and 2000s; Virginia Steele Wood, whose manuscript research on the early history of Darien and McIntosh County finds many citations in my books; the late Anne McKinley King of Milledgeville, one of the finest people I have ever known, encouraged my work and made available to me the Sapelo Reconstruction era journal of her ancestor, Archibald Carlisle

McKinley—the subject of one my recent books; the late Cornelia Walker Bailey of Sapelo Island, my generational contemporary, was a friend and frequent fount of information about the Geechee culture of Sapelo—many were the conversation we had in her home or beneath a shade tree in her yard at Hog Hammock during my twenty-five years on Sapelo; my long-time, friend, neighbor and former Sapelo Island colleague Aimee G. Gaddis has always been supportive of my work and her knowledge of many aspects of coastal history has been invaluable to me; the late Jingle Davis of St. Simons Island, long-time friend and newspaper colleague whose wonderful books about St. Simons, Jekyll and tabby provided the inspiration, with Ben Galland, for *Sapelo: People and Place*; and what more can I say about the many kindnesses and help afforded me by Bill Jones relevant to the Sapelo and Sea Island Company initiatives of his grandfather, Alfred W. Jones, Sr. and his grandfather's older cousin, Howard Earle Coffin? Most of the archival Sapelo images from his grandfather's collection seen in my books are courtesy of Bill Jones, and the books would be much the less useful without them. Finally, the work done by the late historians Ellis Merton Coulter, professor of history at the University of Georgia for more half a century, and Marmaduke Hamilton Floyd, eminent Savannah architect and researcher, have greatly influenced my work relating to Sapelo Island, Thomas Spalding and antebellum tabby buildings.

Meanwhile, my associations with the Georgia Historical Society (Savannah), Coastal Georgia Historical Society (St. Simons Island), Lower Altamaha Historical Society (Darien), Sapelo Island NERR, the *Darien News,* and the Ashantilly Center (Darien), have been rewarding and very satisfying for me over the last forty years, and have enabled lasting friendships with a multitude of people I have been honored to know—Harriet Langford, Lloyd Young Flanders, Bill Haynes, Mattie R. Gladstone, Jeannine and Rundle Cook, Lillian Schaitberger, Maude and Charles Williamson, Kathleen Williamson Russell, Mimi Rogers, Joe Tanner, Malcolm Bell III, Lonice C. Barrett, Dr. David Hurst Thomas, Royce Hayes, Ray Crook, Charles Pearson (who introduced me to the Roswell King journal), Bill Merriman, Stacy Rowe, Genevieve Wynegar, David Bluestein, the late David Earl Lane, Dr. Todd Groce, Dr. Stan Deaton, Walter J. (Jay) Fraser, Esther Shaver, Judy Wood, Roger Smith, Preston Russell, Dr. Martha Keber, Dr. Paul Pressley, Dale Critz, John Inscoe, Lisa White, Swann Seiler, Leslie Long, Christy Sherman, and especially Herb Boyett, a frequent boating companion and historian.

* * *

Departing Sapelo and state government January 1, 2013 enabled me to undertake more research and writing, including a collection of writings in *A Georgia Tidewater Companion*; a monograph on the acquisition by Northerners of the coastal islands after the Civil War, and how these acquisitions led to the later movement to conserve and protect Georgia's coast; the revision of *Early Days* previously mentioned; a biography and collection of the writings of county historian Bessie Lewis; *Sapelo: People and Place on a Georgia Sea Island*, a comprehensive semi-scholarly review of the history of the island complimented by archival images and the striking contemporary photographs of Benjamin Galland.

Sapelo: People and Place on a Georgia Sea Island is undoubtedly my most visually appealing book with its striking color photographs and oversized format and, I think, one of the best researched, organized and written. The University of Georgia Press, one of the outstanding university presses in America, produced a strikingly attractive volume with high-quality formatting and paper stock. This book evolved largely as the result of my work on Sapelo Island from 1993 to 2013 as director of the National Estuarine Research Reserve. Departing the *Darien News* and a 22-year newspaper career in the summer of 1993 for a major mid-life career change on Sapelo opened new opportunities and venues for the development of my research and writing. Being regularly and necessarily exposed to the tangible elements of the history I was writing about made Sapelo the ideal platform on which to expand my research horizons and curiosities.

Environmental Influences on Life & Labor in McIntosh County, an economic history of the county as influenced by ecological considerations, was issued in large format hardcover edition in 2018 followed by a non-illustrated softcover edition in 2020. A companion book to all my previous work, *Atlas of McIntosh County History: A Survey Through Maps & A Personal Commentary*, was published in 2021. It incorporates my personal observations based on a lifetime of exploring the roads and waterways of the county, while investigating its history and ecology. Most of the observations and insights from my experiences on the water are included in the next chapter of the present book, partly drawn from the *Atlas*, with additional thoughts. Another recent work is *Notes from Low Country Georgia: History, Ecology & Perspective*, a compilation (as is the present book) of my writings since 1985. Another book, *Child Life on the Tidewater: A Memoir of Coastal Georgia*, was published in 2021. It includes the memoir that is the present chapter of the present volume, which in essence is an updated version of the first edition.

Incorporating materials from previous studies, I embarked on a new, and different, initiative during the Covid-19 pandemic when speaking engagements were at a standstill and I was largely in a stay-at-home mode. I compiled a nine-volume set of books, issued by BookBaby in a uniform 6 x 9 design format, under separate titles on various aspects of local and coastal history—archaeological investigations of the Native American and Spanish periods, the county's ecological characteristics, a 500-plus history of Darien (the first time Darien has ever had a single, comprehensive volume devoted solely to its history), Blackbeard Island history, a book of stories of the early families of the county up to 1861, Harris Neck and north McIntosh County history, and my favorite, mentioned earlier, *Postbellum Sapelo Island: The Reconstruction Journal of Archibald Carlisle McKinley*, with greatly more detailed documentation contained from an earlier version of the journal by a previous editor. This book led to an extremely rewarding day spent on Sapelo Island in March 2023 with descendants of A.C. McKinley and their families.

Then, published in September 2023, after eighteen months of intensive work, I published what I consider my "definitive" book relevant to McIntosh County and other aspects of coastal history. *Low Country Historian: A Collective Omnibus* is an 840-page large format book with a synthesis of all my best work with additional updates through new findings, and corrections to improve and modify material in previous books. *Low Country Historian*, I feel, is the most complete work I have done on the county within a single volume—it includes an abbreviated memoir from what appears in this book, along with most of the maps from the *Historical Atlas*. I said when that effort was "put to bed" that it would be the "ultimate" book, meaning my last one, the "finale," "coda" or whatever other appellative might be applied in that context. But then the creative urges came back a few months later (do they ever end?) and I have decided that a single book devoted purely to personal reminiscences and career anecdotes would be appropriate primarily for, as pointed out in the preface here, family, extended family, and special friends. Herein is the most detailed memoir of those that appeared in earlier books, including more family images.

As noted, my associations with the Georgia Historical Society from 1996 to 2010 as a member of the board of curators and committee chair, and the Coastal Georgia Historical Society, as

Georgia Historical Society awards luncheon, 2010. The author, center, with his friends Bill Jones III, left. and Dr. Todd Groce, president and CEO of GHS. The award for is for my voluntary contributions to GHS.

Senior Historian, 2014 to the present, have played important roles in my development as a historian of the coast as well as both providing important and useful venues for the preponderance of my research of primary manuscript source materials.

Meanwhile, the result of the Sapelo experience was the preparation of books and monographs that expanded upon my interest in how the local ecosystem affected the lives of the people who have lived here—agriculturally, commercially, socially and culturally—and solidified my conviction of the uniqueness of those intangible elements of "place" and "permanence" to the people, not just of Sapelo, but to all those whose generational roots are firmly rooted in the coastal low country. Thus, the thematic approach to my published works since 2006 or so has been to relate the economic, agricultural and maritime history of the Georgia coast from an ecological perspective, i.e., how local environmental circumstances and conditions, both ashore and afloat, have shaped people's lives, and how they made their living. I have used stories of how people utilized and worked the land in tandem with the ecosystem, stories of "land use and landscape," and of "life and labor" on the tidewater as viewed through the prism of ecology. My awareness of the nuances of coastal ecosystems and how they fit in with how people have adapted to them, and lived and worked amid them, comes from my childhood and adolescence on the McIntosh County tidewater. It was then that my impressions of *ecology as history*, as well as the significance of low country *place* and *permanence* evolved to fruition in my writings such as the ecological review of the region in the next chapter of this book. Concomitantly, I believe my research instincts, and my writing and book organizational skills, have consistently improved over the years—particularly so since my former newspaper days when writing on pressing deadlines often compromised my preference to preserve the sanctity of the Queen's English. Similarly, some of my best works have evolved from projects upon which I entered with little or no knowledge of the subject. The best example of this is my history of Bryan County, Georgia, *From Beautiful Zion to Red Bird Creek* (2000), a volume that is arguably the best combination of research, use of primary sources, book organization and writing expression of any volume I have done, with the possible exception of the recent *Low Country Historian.* Residing in Richmond Hill from 1995 to 2018 (with daily commutes to work at Sapelo) greatly enhanced my producing that book.

My perspective on the flow of McIntosh County and coastal Georgia history reflects this ongoing interest in *ecology as history* from several topical approaches: an understanding of the dynamics of salt marsh ecology, and the estuarine science employed in understanding it; what ecology and archaeology have told us about the way people lived a thousand years in the past; the use of the land by generations of its owners; tideflow rice cultivation utilizing fresh water and tidal systems; agriculture in a barrier island environment; the influence of waterways—fresh and salt—in the development of a coastal maritime legacy, including the commercial oyster and shrimp fisheries; ecology as history in its relevance to the interior pine flatwoods in the conduct of naval stores production; and, finally, studies relating to the twentieth century coast—uplands, islands, marshes and tidal waterways—and the evolving efforts within these systems toward attaining scientific understanding and, equally-importantly, advocating the responsible stewardship of our local natural resources. Thus, the work goes on and, as I write this at the age of seventy-seven, I still have lost none of my energy, passion and enthusiasm for continuing to document, record and, in some small way, to help conserve and protect our beautiful Georgia coast.

Some Closing Visual Images of Home in the Low Country:
No Other Place on Earth Quite Like It...

Moonrise over the marshlands of the coastal low country.

Sea oats and dunes at Nanny Goat Beach, Sapelo Island.

Sunset at Cedar Point, two perspectives across the marsh to Baisden's Bluff and Crescent.

Summer sky and tidal marsh, the essence of the coastal low country.

Sunset over the marshes at Cedar Point. Image by the author used as the cover of the first edition of *Child-Life on the Tidewater* (2021)

Author's Genealogy

Including Johnson Family Ties to 1955

Paternal Great-Great-Grandparents

William Manning Sullivan (b. 3 March 1828, Leesburg, Lee County, Ga., d.
26 September 1883, Camilla, Mitchell County, Ga.) m. (1848) Rebecca
Jane Shiver (b. 4 October 1827, Dooly County, Ga., d. 30 April
1912, Camilla, Mitchell County, Ga.). Parents of Henry Wilburn Sullivan.
Henry Calloway Holt (1831-1870) m. Samantha Pearl (Martha) Blanchett
(1839-1892). Parents of Ellen Ethel Holt Sullivan.
Joseph Milton Sumner (b. 16 August 1836, Sumner, Worth County, Ga., d.
25 December 1913, Sumner, Worth County, Ga.) m. (1858) Elizabeth
Jane Young (b. 15 February 1841, Irwin County, Ga., d. 1 March 1930,
Sumner, Worth County, Ga.). Parents of Frances Nell Sumner Lemon.
Duncan Malcolm Lemon (1819-1889) m. Sarah Ann Currie (1828-1898).
Parents of Malcolm Currie Lemon.

Maternal Great-Great-Grandparents

Miles Hill Hunter (b. 8 November 1834, Charlotte County, Va., d. 29 March
1914, Chester, South Carolina) m. (1) Margaret Kalista Patterson (b.
1838, d. 1860?, Newberry, South Carolina); m. (2) (1867) Sallie Marshall
(b. 1847, d. 5 June 1891, Chester, South Carolina). A son, Thomas
Marshall Hunter, was born in 1870 in the second marriage.
Benjamin Howard Owen (b. 9 April 1849, Lebanon, Wilson County, Tenn.,
d. 17 August 1940, Charleston, S.C.) m. (1870) Mary Beta Kennedy
(Bryan?) (1851-1924). Parents of Sallie Owen Hunter.
Needham Thomas Johnson (b. 1831, Houston County, Ga., d. 1893, Pulaski
County, Ga.) m. Sarah M. Holmes (b. 1835, Houston County, Ga., d.
1904, Houston County, Ga.). Parents of Henry Herbert Johnson.
John Calhoun Wheeler (b. 1840, East Carroll Parish, La., d. 1891, Macon,
Bibb County, Ga.) m. Mary Anola Polhill, b. 1845, Louisville, Ga., d.
1931, Crescent, McIntosh County, Ga.). Parents of Wilhelmina
Wheeler Johnson.

Paternal Great-Grandparents:

Henry Wilburn Sullivan (b. 13 May 1860, Mitchell County, Ga., d. 30 March 1943, Decatur County, Ga., buried, Vada, Ga.) m. (1880) Ellen Ethel Holt (b. 25 February 1862, Decatur County, Ga., d. 3 January 1935, Bainbridge, Decatur County, Ga., buried, Vada, Ga.). Parents of Harvey Leroy Sullivan.

Malcolm Currie Lemon (b. 22 September 1855, Moore, N.C., d. 10 November 1901, Sumner, Worth County, Ga., buried, Sumner) m. (1887) Frances Nell Sumner (b. 15 June 1865, Sumner, Worth County, Ga., d. 17 January 1940, Sumner, Worth County, buried, Sumner, Ga.). Parents of Wilma Frances Lemon Sullivan.

Maternal Great-Grandparents:

Thomas Marshall Hunter (b. 7 April 1870, Chester, S.C., d. September 1937, Beaumont, Texas, buried, Baton Rouge, La.) m. (1894) Sallie Owen (b. Clarkesville, Tenn., 3 February 1872, d. 15 December 1959, buried, Baton Rouge, La.). Parents of Howard Owen Hunter.

Henry Herbert Johnson (b. 11 November 1861, Hawkinsville, Pulaski County, Ga., d. 23 May 1937, Crescent, McIntosh County, Ga., buried, Macon, Ga.) m. (1897) Wilhelmina Wheeler (b. 16 August 1872, Georgia, d. 1 July 1955, Chatham County, Ga., buried, Darien, Ga.). Adoptive parents (unsubstantiated) of Mary Emily Jane Jackson Hunter. NOTE: No information has been available to date on the ancestry of Mary Emily Jane Jackson, natural maternal grandmother of the author.

Paternal Grandparents:

Harvey Leroy (Roy) Sullivan (b. 20 March 1893, Mitchell County, Ga., d. 22 December 1967, Tifton, Tift County, Ga., buried, Tifton, Ga.) m. (1920) Wilma Frances Lemon (b. 20 March 1900, Sumner, Worth County, Ga., d. 1 October 1986, Columbus, Muscogee County, Ga., buried, Tifton, Ga.). Parents of Roy Earl Sullivan.

88

Maternal Grandparents:

Howard Owen Hunter (b. 25 July 1895, Darien, McIntosh County, Ga., d. 22 February 1964, Fort Lauderdale, Broward County, Fla., buried, Baton Rouge, La.) m. (1) (1920) Mary Emily Jane Jackson (b. 8 January 1893, Tenn., d. 1 May 1968, Quitman, Brooks County, Ga., buried, St. Andrew Cemetery, Darien, Ga.), divorced 1933. Parents of Mary Kate Hunter Sullivan; m. (2) Marjory Lichty, divorced, n.d.; m. (3) (1945) Edna McNabb (b. 6 December 1913, Dothan, Ala., d. 9 March 2004, Fort Lauderdale, Broward County, Fla., cremated).

Parents:

Roy Earl Sullivan (b. 14 January 1921, Sumner, Worth County, Ga., d. 2 September 2016, Johnson City, Washington County, Tenn., buried, Riverdale Cemetery, Columbus, Ga.) m. (1) (1945, Atlanta, Ga.) Mary Kate Hunter (b. 24 May 1924, Macon, Ga., d. 14 February 1954, Washington, D.C., buried, St. Andrew Cemetery, Darien, Ga.); m. (2) (1955, Fort Benning, Ga.) Alcye Lois Streetman (b. 18 June 1932-). A daughter, Karen Ann Sullivan, b. 21 July 1961 to the second marriage.

Roy Earl Sullivan, Jr. (Buddy)

b. 29 July 1946, Savannah, Chatham County, Ga. m (1) (1970, Alexandria, Va.) Martha Ellen Silberhorn (1948-2019), divorced 1979; m. (2) (1981, LaGrange, Ga.) Sharon Rebecca Daniel Hammock (1957-), LaGrange, Ga., divorced 1994.

Children:

Kenneth Patrick Sullivan, b. 30 June 1971, Columbus, Muscogee County, Ga., m. Shannon Marie Oliver, 13 November 2004, Atlanta, Fulton County, Ga., with one child, Emma Frances Sullivan, b. 24 September 2007, Atlanta, Fulton County, Ga.

Teri Lynn Hammock Sullivan, b. 30 September 1978, LaGrange, Troup County, Ga., m. Charles Harold Fischer III, 22 June 2002, Atlanta, Fulton County, Ga., with two children, Charles Harold Fischer IV, b. 5 January 2007, Lawrenceville, Gwinnett County, Ga., and Cadee Grace Fischer, b. 15 May 2009, Atlanta, Fulton County, Ga.

Amanda Kate Sullivan Wilson, b. 20 August 1983, Savannah, Chatham County, Ga., m. Hugh McColl Wilson, Jr., 24 November 2007, Charleston, S.C.

Sister

Karen Ann Sullivan (b. 21 July 1961, Columbus, Muscogee County, Ga.) m. Robert Rule Sams, (b. 1957, Tenn.), 11 August 1990, Roswell, Fulton County, Ga., with one child, Stephanie Kay Sams, b. 4 April 1992, Johnson City, Washington County, Tenn.

Buddy Sullivan:
Career Notes & Bibliography

Author and consultant specializing in coastal Georgia history.
Retired manager, Sapelo Island National Estuarine Research Reserve, 1993 to 2013.
Native of McIntosh County, Georgia.
Columbus (GA) High School, 1964.
LaGrange College (BA History), 1968.
Residences: Cedar Point, McIntosh County (1946-51); Sendai, Japan (1951-52); Columbus, GA (1952-53); Cedar Point, McIntosh County (1953-55); Schofield Barracks, Hawaii (1955-57); Columbus, GA (1957); Cedar Point, McIntosh County (1958-60); Columbus, GA (1960-66, with summer months at Cedar Point, McIntosh County); LaGrange, GA (1966-69), Fort Belvoir, VA (1969-71), Hopewell, VA (1971); Columbus, GA (1971-73); Jacksonville, FL (1973); LaGrange, GA (1974-82), Savannah, GA (1982-85); Kittles Island, McIntosh County (1985-95); Sapelo Island, GA (1995-96); Richmond Hill, GA (1996-2018); Cedar Point, McIntosh County (2018-present).

Organizations

Georgia Historical Society, Savannah, Board of Curators, 1996-2010.

Lower Altamaha Historical Society, Darien, President, 1996-2000, 2014-18.

Richmond Hill Historical Society, President, 1997-2001.

Ashantilly Center, Inc. Board of Directors, 2013-present (2024).

Senior Historian, Coastal Georgia Historical Society, St. Simons Island, 2014-present (2024).

United States Naval Institute, Annapolis, MD, 1983-present.

Professional

LaGrange (GA) Daily News, Sports Writer, 1967-68.

LaGrange Daily News, Sports Editor, 1968-69.

US Army, Clerk, Department of Recreation, Fort Belvoir, VA, 1969-71.

Alexandria (VA) Gazette, Sports Writer, 1970-71.

Petersburg (VA) Progress-Index, Sports Writer, 1971.

Columbus (GA) Enquirer, Assistant Sports Editor, 1971-73.

Florida Times-Union (Jacksonville), Sports Writer, 1973.

LaGrange Daily News, Sports Editor, 1974-82.

Savannah Morning News, Assistant Sports Editor, 1982-85.

Darien (GA) News, Editor, 1985-93.

Sapelo Island National Estuarine Research Reserve, Manager, 1993-2013.

Private consultant, lecturer, and researcher, 2013-present (2024).

Other (as volunteer):

Senior Historian, Coastal Georgia Historical Society (2014-present); Lecturer: series in coastal Georgia history for Brunswick College, 1989-93; Coastal Georgia Historical Society, 1994-present; coastal history series The Learning Center, Senior Center, Savannah.

Publications

Books (in order of publication)

Dress Her in Orange and Blue, The Story of Columbus High, the Bi-City and Georgia Prep Sports, 1908-1975 (Columbus, GA, 1976).

Hunker Down: The Story of Dooley's Dogs, 1964-1980 (self-published, 1981).

A History of the Darien Presbyterian Church (First Presbyterian Church, Darien, GA, 1986).

Sapelo: A History (Georgia Department of Natural Resources, Atlanta, 1988-2020.

The Darien Bank: A Celebration of One Hundred Years (The Darien Bank, Darien, GA, 1989).

Memories of McIntosh (Darien News, Darien, GA, 1990).

Early Days on the Georgia Tidewater, The Story of McIntosh County and Sapelo (McIntosh County Board of Commissioners, Darien, GA, six editions, 1990-2001).

From Beautiful Zion to Red Bird Creek, A History of Bryan County, Georgia (Bryan County Board of Commissioners, Pembroke, GA, 2000).

Sapelo Island (Tempus Publishing, Charleston, SC, 2000).

Darien and McIntosh County, Georgia (Tempus Publishing, Charleston, SC, 2000).

Georgia: A State History (Tempus Publishing, sponsored by Georgia Historical Society, 2003).

"All Under Bank," Roswell King, Jr., and Plantation Management in Tidewater Georgia, 1819-1854 (Liberty County Historical Society, 2003, reissued by Midway Museum Board of Governors, 2013).

Richmond Hill (Tempus Publishing, Charleston, SC., 2006).

High Water on the Bar: An Operational Perspective of a Tidewater Timber Port, with the Memoirs of Thomas Hilton and Minutes of the Darien Pilot Commissioners, 1874-1930 (Darien, GA, 2009).

The Darien Journal of John Girardeau Legare, Ricegrower (Athens: University of Georgia Press, 2010). New edition of original edition published in 1997 by the City of Darien.

A Georgia Tidewater Companion: Essays, Papers and Some Personal Observations On 30 Years of Research in Coastal Georgia History (privately published, 2014).

A Low Country Diary: Bessie Mary Lewis and McIntosh County, Georgia (Lower Altamaha Historical Society, 2016).

Sapelo: People and Place on a Georgia Sea Island (Athens: University of Georgia Press, 2017).

Early Days on the Georgia Tidewater, A New Revised Edition (privately published, 2018).

Environmental Influences on Life & Labor in McIntosh County, Georgia (privately published, 2018).

Thomas Spalding, Antebellum Planter of Sapelo (privately published, 2019).

Life & Labor on Butler's Island: Rice Cultivation in the Altamaha Delta (privately published, 2019).

Blackbeard Island: A History (privately published, 2019).

Native American & Spanish Influences on McIntosh County, Georgia: An Archaeological Perspective (privately published, 2019).

Darien, Georgia: A History of the Town & Its Environs (privately published, 2020).

Harris Neck & Its Environs: Land Use & Landscape in North McIntosh County, Georgia (privately published, 2020).

Twentieth Century Sapelo Island: Howard E. Coffin & Richard J. Reynolds, Jr. (privately published, 2020).

Early Families of McIntosh County, Georgia, 1736-1861 (privately published, 2020).

Postbellum Sapelo Island: The Reconstruction Journal of Archibald Carlisle McKinley (privately published, 2020).

Notes from Low Country Georgia: History, Ecology & Perspective (privately published, 2020).

Child-Life on the Tidewater: A Memoir of Coastal Georgia (privately published, 2020). 1st edition.

Environmental Influences on Life & Labor in McIntosh County, Georgia, revised softcover edition, (privately published, 2020).

Historical Atlas of McIntosh County, Georgia, A Survey Through Maps & a Personal Commentary (privately published, 2021).

Low Country Historian: A Collective Omnibus (privately published, 2023).

Child-Life on the Tidewater: A Memoir of Coastal Georgia (privately published, 2024). 2nd edition. (The present volume).

Monographs

Williamsburg, Georgia & the Williams Family: Their Place in Time, privately published by the Williams family, 1989.

The Hurricane and Tidal Wave of 1898 in McIntosh County, Georgia, Lower Altamaha Historical Society, 1998.

The Lighthouses of Georgia, Coastal Museum of St. Simons Island and Georgia, Georgia Department of Natural Resources, 2002 (2nd edition).

Cotton Port on the Altamaha: A Historical and Archaeological Perspective of the Darien, Georgia Waterfront, Lower Altamaha Historical Society, 2002.

Tabby: A Historical Perspective of an Antebellum Building Material in McIntosh County, Georgia, Lower Altamaha Historical Society 2002.

The First Conservationists? Northern Money and Low Country Georgia, 1866-1930, Charleston, SC, 2016.

"Old Tabby": The Ashantilly Legacy of Thomas Spalding and William G. Haynes, The Ashantilly Center, Inc., 2018.

Book Contributions

Family Histories of McIntosh County, LeVerne Gardner, ed., 1992. Compiler of historical narrative of county history.

The New Georgia Guide (University of Georgia Press, Athens, 1996). Author of coastal Georgia historical tour section.

Cemeteries of McIntosh County, Mattie R. Gladstone, et. al., eds. (Darien, Ga.: Lower Altamaha Historical Society, 2000). Introduction and historical background.

They Called Their Town Darien (Darien, Ga.: Lower Altamaha Historical Society, 2002). New Introduction comprising a biographical sketch of the late author Bessie Mary Lewis.

The New Georgia Encyclopedia (University of Georgia, Athens), ongoing from 2003. Writer of 14 essays on various coastal Georgia topics.

Papers

"The Lighthouses of Georgia," in *The Keeper's Log*, Journal of the United States Lighthouse Society, Spring 1988.

"Historical Background of Lots 1 and 2 on the Darien, Georgia, Waterfront," in *An Historical, Archaeological and Architectural Study of the Darien, Georgia Waterfront*, Cultural Resources Mitigation of State Site 9McI367, McIntosh County Development Authority, 1991.

"Tabby: A Historical Perspective of an Antebellum Building Material in McIntosh County, Georgia," in *Proceedings of a Symposium on the Conservation and Preservation of Tabby*, Historic Preservation Department, GDNR, 1999.

"Ecology as History in the Sapelo Island National Estuarine Research Reserve," Sapelo Island NERR, Occasional Papers, (1) 2008.

"The Historic Buildings of Sapelo: A 200-Year Architectural Legacy," Sapelo Island NERR, Occasional Papers, (2), 2010.

"Sapelo Island Settlement and Land Ownership: A Historical Overview, 1865-1970," Sapelo Island NERR, Occasional Papers, (3), 2012.

Book Reviews

"The North American Journal of Edward Kimber, 1741-1743," in *Georgia Historical Quarterly*, Fall 1998.

"Rice Gold: James Hamilton Couper and Antebellum Georgia," in *Georgia Historical Quarterly*, Summer 2000.

"Dear Roswell: Civil War Letters of the King Family," in *Georgia Historical Quarterly*, Spring 2004.

"Lowcountry Hurricanes: Three Centuries of Storms at Sea and Ashore," in *Georgia Historical Quarterly* (Spring 2009).

"Hell's Broke Loose in Georgia: Survival in a Civil War Regiment," in *Georgia Historical Quarterly*, Summer 2009.

"Guardian of Savannah" (Fort McAllister), in *Georgia Historical Quarterly*, Summer 2010.

"Steam Coffin" (S.S. Savannah), in *Georgia Historical Quarterly*, Spring 2013.

"Island Time: An Illustrated History of St. Simons Island, Georgia," in *Georgia Historical Quarterly*, Spring 2014.

Awards and Honors

Certificate of Commendation, American Association for State and Local History, 1999, from Coastal Georgia Historical Society.

Jefferson Davis Gold Medal from Georgia United Daughters of the Confederacy, for contributions to the advancement of Confederate military history, 2000.

National History Award Medal, Daughters of the American Revolution, for contributions to the advancement of Georgia history, 2000.

Lilla M. Hawes Award from the Georgia Historical Society for the outstanding book in Georgia on local history published in 2000, for the history of Bryan County.

Recipient of the Governor's Medal in the Humanities from the Georgia Humanities Council, 2005, in recognition of contributions to the "understanding, preservation and teaching of the history of the State of Georgia."

Recipient of the Sarah Nichols Pinckney Volunteer Award for service to the Georgia Historical Society, 2010.

Lifetime Achievement Award, Lower Altamaha Historical Society, 2010.

Selected Lectures

"Postbellum Sapelo Island," Annual Meeting of the Coastal Georgia Historical Society, Sea Island, Georgia, January 1991.

"Columbus and the Land of Ayllon," Lecture Commemorating the 500th Anniversary of the Discovery of the New World, Darien, September 1992 at Symposium sponsored by Lower Altamaha Historical Society and Georgia Historical Society.

"The Spanish in Coastal Georgia," Georgia Historical Society, Savannah, November 1992.

"Coastal Georgia in the New Georgia Guide," Annual Meeting of the Georgia Historical Society, Savannah, April 1996.

"Rice Production on the Georgia Tidewater," Georgia Historical Society, Savannah, 1997.

"Antebellum Coastal Georgia and Roswell, Georgia" Roswell Historical Society, May 1997.

"Rice Plantations: Thomas County's Coastal Georgia Connection," Fall Meeting of The Georgia Historical Society, Thomasville, September 1998.

"Early Settlers of Colonial Coastal Georgia: Scots, Puritans and English Royalists, 1733-1775," Georgia Humanities Council, Tignall, Georgia, May 2000.

"From Beautiful Zion to Red Bird Creek: Savannah and Bryan County, Georgia," Georgia Historical Society, Savannah, 2000.

"Sapelo and Ossabaw Islands: Coffins, Torreys & the Unique Connection," Ossabaw Island Foundation, Savannah, January 2003.

"Georgia: A State History," Georgia Historical Society, Savannah, 2003; similar lectures in Augusta and Columbus, 2003, 2004.

"Roswell King and Plantation Management in Tidewater, 1819-1854," Georgia Historical Society, Savannah, 2005.

"Life, Labor and Landscape on the Georgia Coast," The Georgia Conservancy and the Coastal Heritage Society, Savannah, 2006; and Symposium on Vernacular Architecture, Savannah College of Art & Design, Savannah, 2007.

"Far Ahead of His Time: The Remarkable Thomas Spalding," Annual Meeting of the Coastal Georgia Historical Society, St. Simons Island, January 2007.

"African Americans on the Georgia Tidewater: Their Cultural and Historical Legacy," Symposium on African American Culture in Coastal Georgia 18th to 20th Centuries, Ossabaw Island Foundation, Savannah, February 2008.

"The Lower Altamaha Historical Society: Reflections Upon Its Past, and Some Observations on Its Present & Future," Address on the commemoration of the 30th anniversary of the Society, Darien, Georgia, October 25, 2009.

"Oglethorpe and the Defense of the Georgia Colony in the Summer of 1742," National Society of Colonial Wars, Savannah Chapter, Savannah, 2010.

"John Couper, the Couper Family and Cannon's Point, St. Simons Island," Coastal Georgia Historical Society, St. Simons Island, 2011.

"John McIntosh Kell of the CSS *Alabama* and the Kell Family of Darien, Georgia," The Ashantilly Center, Darien, 2012.

"Antebellum Darien and McIntosh County, 1800-1861," Lecture series commemorating the 150th anniversary of the burning of Darien, Darien, May 2013.

"The Burning of Darien: We Know the How, But What About the Why?" Lecture series commemorating the 150th anniversary of the burning of Darien, Darien, June 2013.

"The Naval War of 1812: America and the Early Republic Navy," Navy League of the United States, Savannah Chapter, Savannah, February 2013.

"Southern Timber for Tall Ships: Georgia Place Names and the Naval War of 1812," Georgia Historical Society, Savannah, June 2014.

"Howard Earle Coffin: Visionary for Early Twentieth Century Coastal Georgia," Coastal Georgia Historical Society, St. Simons Island and Sea Island, August and September 2014.

"Sapelo: People and Place on a Georgia Sea Island," (discussing new book, Savannah, St. Simons, Darien, 2016-2017.

"The First Conservationists? Northern Money and the Georgia Sea
Islands, 1880-1930," Symposium on the cultural history of coastal
Georgia from an ecological perspective, Savannah, Ossabaw
Island Foundation, February 2016.
"Environmental Influences on Life & Labor in Coastal Georgia,"
The Ashantilly Center, January 2018.
"Richmond Hill: 200 Years, 1750-1950," Richmond Hill Visitors
and Convention Bureau and Richmond Hill Historical Society,
Richmond Hill, Georgia, February 2020.
"The City by the Sea: A History of Brunswick, Georgia," Coastal
Georgia Historical Society, Brunswick, October 2021.

Collections—Buddy Sullivan Papers, Collection 2433, Georgia
Historical Society, Savannah. Personal correspondence, maps and
charts, books and the accumulated notes, papers and documents
accrued from 1968 to 2013 relating to professional career and
research in the history of coastal Georgia, particularly that of
Bryan, Liberty and McIntosh counties, and Sapelo, St. Simons
and Ossabaw islands.

Investigations & Explorations

A Personal Connection: Tidal Waters & History

My published histories of McIntosh and Bryan counties, in addition to a state history of Georgia, and books on various specialized subjects, all reflect an abundance of maps, charts and surveys. As my maturity as a historian developed, I began to more and more make the obvious connection between the disciplines of cartography—maps—and the ecological circumstances of a given locale. Thus evolved my increasing attention to the importance of the influence of ecology and environment upon local history from the standpoint of economic developments, be they agricultural, timber and naval stores, or commercial fisheries, all the ways in which the people of McIntosh County and tidewater Georgia have defined their lives and livelihoods.

The discussion that follows evolved from my map research going back to my adolescence, improved by more disciplined investigations during the research for my books about the coast, and all of it complemented by numerous excursions on McIntosh County and coastal Georgia waterways in an assortment of boats—from manual (usually laborious) oar-propelled pine bateaux, to a variety of outboard engine-powered craft, to occasional forays on shrimp boats over the years. The discussion of my association with boats and the tidal waters of the county in the opening chapter of this book makes it very clear that some of the best times of my life have been those spent on the waterways.

Much of the anecdotal material in this chapter is extracted from the notes contained in my book *Historical Atlas of McIntosh County, Georgia.* It reflects my personal observations and experiences gleaned from many explorations around McIntosh County, both by water and land, particularly with respect to the familiar areas in the eastern section of the county—Cedar Point, Valona, Belleville, and Pine Harbor, among other locales. The maps in the *Atlas,* and in *Low Country Historian,* may be consulted for the necessary cartographic context in the discussions that follow in this chapter.

Early Adolescent Explorations

In the summer of 1963, as a sixteen-year-old, I took it upon myself to record my impressions of the local waterways on which I often traveled, being already cognizant and acutely aware of the special nature of our ecosystem: marshes, waters and islands. There was also my growing sense of McIntosh history. The following, un-edited, is what I wrote then. I had no idea then that I would eventually turn to writing as a professional, whether in the realms of newspaper reporting, or writing books of history. For this and other water excursions I was using my 12-foot aluminum boat powered by a 10-horsepower Evinrude outboard motor. It was an extremely serviceable craft for the years of my adolescence and a lot of nautical miles were put on it along the inland tidal waters of McIntosh County.

* * *

Cedar Creek–Settlement of *Cedar Point* situated upon. Empties into Crescent River. A depth of 6 feet at low tide can be carried to Amason and Burrows shrimp boat docks about ½ mile from entrance. Private docks along creek until the abandoned oyster factory is reached. This is the last landing on the creek. A depth of 7 feet can be carried to the Point, or Horsehead Bend. The Point is of oaks, cedars and scrub that juts into the marsh. A depth of 2 feet can be carried to Highway 99 at Oak Hill bridge. At this point Cedar Creek winds into a dense swamp.

Crescent River empties into Mud River and Old Teakettle Creek. Depth of 14 feet can be carried to Creighton dock. *Creighton Island* is owned by Will E. Williams of Baisden's Bluff and Frank Williams of Meridian. The island is unpopulated. About three miles in length and a mile wide in the middle. Creighton resembles the hull of a ship when seen from the air. Wide at north end which touches *Back River,* and gradually narrowing to a point at its south end. Landings are on Crescent River on the west and Front River on the east side. Island is heavily wooded on the sides, but a large open meadow is found near the south end. Here cows and hogs roam about. Creighton's extreme southern tip is accessible at high tide by a small creek emptying into Creighton Narrows. A person can step right on to the island at this point, but thick woods grow nearly to the water's edge. Many birds inhabit the trees here. There are many palm trees on the west side, and this gives a peaceful atmosphere to the island.

100

A road runs down the middle of the island from north to south. Creighton was populated by Negroes up until the war. The island was bought by the Williams brothers and used to get pulpwood from it. The island is almost completely surrounded by marsh so a pair of heavy docks were built.

A depth of 3 feet can be carried to *Happy Landing*. A store is located here and gas and bait may be obtained. The Crescent River here is bordered by steep bluffs and marsh. The ruins of Baisden's Bluff Academy overlook the river.

Going back out Crescent River to about ¼ mile before Creighton dock *Rattlesnake Creek* is entered and carries for 1 mile through the marsh to *Sapelo River*. Into Sapelo River the village of *Belleville* is seen. Shrimp docks are the first of a long string of docks. Belleville is a resort place but about 200 people live here. Following the Sapelo River for about 1 mile a depth of 7 feet can be carried to *Pine Harbor*, a resort. Here also are many docks and homes. At Doty's Camp and Moye's Restaurant food, ice and gas may be obtained. Going on for another ¾ mile a depth of 7 feet can be carried to the Buccaneer Club. One may return to the other side of Belleville through Roscoe Cut, a manmade cut.

Creighton Narrows empties into Crescent River at marker 156 on the east side of Creighton Island. A dredged channel permits the use of this and *Front River* at any tide to Sapelo Sound. Several small hammocks are along the river's edge. These are just little islands with two or three cedar or pine trees on them. A depth of 15 feet can be carried through to marker 151. At marker 152 one or two small islands are seen just before entering *Sapelo Sound*. The last of these is *Hazzard's Ballast Pile*. It is a small hammock and there is a thick growth of low trees and vines. It is owned by Jane Atwood. There is an artesian well flowing from the ground through a pipe. At the water's edge many rocks are seen. These are the ballast of ships passing by to get cargoes of lumber at Cedar Point and Valona [sic]. In the 1920s Cedar Point was owned by the Atwoods and a large port thrived there. A telephone was once at Hazzard's and when ships passed by Cedar Point was notified. Henry Atwood named the island for one of the ship captains [sic]. No one lives here now but the tropical growth and birds. The island is about 50 yards long facing the Front River. Many people stop here to fish and to get water from the well.

Proceeding into Sapelo Sound at marker 149 is *Dog Hammock*. There is no land here, only a large point consisting of only marsh.

Dog Hammock Spit extends from here and many shrimp boats have been stranded by grounding.

Back to Crescent River—Old *Teakettle Creek* is deep on the west side but is shallow and there are sand bars on the opposite side. Proceeding to the mouth of *Shellbluff Creek* at marker 162, a depth of 7 feet at low tide can be carried to *Valona*. Here are located Watson's and Durant's shrimp boat docks and a marine railway. Mr. Radford's store and post office are also located here. Gasoline, ice and some food can be obtained. Large oaks face the river beside Watson's docks. Durant's docks are the largest, and from this point on, Shellbluff Creek touches no land. It winds its way ½ a mile or so into the marsh. At high tide small boats can get to Cedar Point through a network of small creeks.

Return to Old Teakettle Creek and proceed south about ½ mile to the first creek on the right. Follow it to the junction of several creeks at the head of Doboy Sound. Take the one on the right which is *Atwood Creek*. After rounding a bend *Patterson Island* is seen. This island has the shape of a hand with the index finger pointing up. The island is about a tenth as large as Creighton. There is a dock and a large house here. Patterson is used as a resort during the summer. Going on, a small island or two are seen on the left bank of the creek. A depth of 14 feet can be carried to the home of Frank Williams Jr. A depth of 3 feet can be carried to the southern end of Valona to the Kittles brothers shrimp docks. The homes of Peter and George Kittles are here. Atwood Creek is unnavigable past the docks.

Return to the mouth of Atwood Creek and proceed south into *Doboy Sound*. At the juncture of Old Teakettle Creek and the sound *Little Sapelo Island* is seen to be wooded by large trees. Further down, at marker 176 near the mouth of *Duplin River, Doboy Island* and *Commodore Island* can be seen. A large house is on Doboy, also docks. This island is wooded, and buildings are on the S.W. end. Part of Doboy is owned by a Mr. Anthony of Macon. A floating dock gives access to the island. Going off the dock a large two-story house faces the [Back] river. There is a nice lawn. Paths have been cut through the marsh to a tiny hammock a little south of the main island of Doboy. Further down Back River is located Commodore Island. This is composed of nine small, wooded hammocks. One of them has a small cottage on it. Following the intracoastal waterway and *North River* small islands [Rock Island] are observed with cabins on some of them. Proceeding further on North River a large island is observed. This is *Hird Island* owned by C.C. Stebbins of Darien. The island is

1½ miles long and ½ mile wide. No one lives here. There are cattle and wild hogs though. Also, an artesian well at the north end. A depth of 14 feet can be carried for 1 mile to *Union Island,* a small island with trees and growth. Ruins of a large red brick stack is observed on Union Island, also remains of docks. It is owned by John Pack of Darien and is used for hog grazing. A depth of 15 feet can be carried around the bend of North River to Blue and Hall a popular swimming place for the people of Darien and the Ridge. A small restaurant is here. Go south to *Black Island Creek.* Shallow at low water and very winding. Passes by *Pine Island* which is small. Creek winds for ¾ mile to *Black Island.* It is about the size of Hird Island. Owned by Paul Varner. Uninhabited but is used for cutting pulpwood. A sawmill is located on the island. Creek carries for 2 miles to *Darien River.*

A shrimp boat experience I had as an adult—while still a sports writer in LaGrange, Georgia—occurred in the summer of 1975 while on a visit to my maternal uncle H.O. (Owen) Hunter, Jr., and his wife, Wanda Atwood Hunter. Owen owned the *Orion,* a handsome 60-foot, double-outrigger, diesel-powered trawler, homeported at Valona, within sight of the Hunter's home there on the bluff of Shellbluff Creek. Owen treated me to a day on his vessel operated by his two highly proficient shrimp fishing employees, both African American with traditional ancestral roots in the McIntosh County fishing industry. What follows is an extract from a lengthy article I published soon after, in August 1975, in the *LaGrange Daily News,* and later reprinted by Charles Williamson in the *Darien News.*

"...To understand the industry, you have to understand the shrimp. It's not a complicated process because nature dictates most of the policy. Shrimp spawn in the ocean then migrate early in their life to the tidal creeks and marshes. The shrimp feed on plankton from the blankets of coastal marsh. There, they develop and mature before moving back into the sea where they reach full size for catching...The weather has a lot to do with good shrimping, which explains why the industry can be such a fickle one. A lot of rain means a bad situation for the shrimpers. When too much fresh water enters the estuary where the young shrimp are maturing it impedes their development. Shrimpers don't like to see a lot of rain—quite the converse from land-bound farmers who do. Shrimpers also like to see a stiff northeasterly breeze, which augers well for good shrimping at sea...The care and maintenance of the boats runs into a lot of money.

Paint, cordage, lines, nets, hull repairs and engine room upkeep can be expensive. Nets can run into the hundreds of dollars and the boats usually require twice a year haul-outs on the marine railway for bottom cleaning and service...Up Sapelo and Blackbeard offshore, then down again as the nets drag the ocean bottom. Running 15 to 20 knots at top speed with the nets inboard, the pull exerted by the dragging trawl slows the vessel to a crawl. A powerful diesel engine is required for the severe strain...Chris, our captain, decides one drag today is enough with the fishing so poor—it would only mean more wasted fuel. The other boats in our area have similar thoughts and are beginning to head for port after one or two drags...Re-entering Doboy Sound enroute to Valona, past Sapelo light on gentle swells with a brilliant sun overhead, we are followed by hundreds of gulls and pelicans, the scavengers of the deep...Tomorrow Chris will fish the *Orion* in a different area in hopes of better luck. He is waiting for early September and the end of dog days when summer catches are typically poor..."

Tidal & Upland Explorations

The era of *Franciscan missions* on the Georgia coast has always held fascination for historians and archaeologists. Authorities in Spanish Florida administered the Province of Guale, later the English colony of Georgia, with the establishment of missions to educate and convert the Guale Indians to Christianity. Three of the 17th-century missions were in what became McIntosh County. Tolomato was likely on the upper end of Harris Neck, San Joseph de Sapala was on Sapelo Island, and Santo Domingo Talaje was at Lower Bluff west of the later town of Darien. These missions worked to Christianize the Guale Indian populations of the coast for over one hundred years before English incursions from the new colony of South Carolina ultimately forced the Spanish to gradually abandon their missions in the 1680s and relocate them to Florida. The missions are a fascinating part of our history. In the summer of 2013, I personally visited the site of Santa Catalina de Guale on St. Catherines Island where David H. Thomas of New York had conducted archaeological field research for thirty-five years. Sitting there on a wooden bench amid what was once the first church in what became Georgia was one of the most revelatory and moving personal experiences I had had in my years of research. It truly was experiencing history at first hand. As for Sapelo, it remains unclear as to the precise location of the mission there. Was it perhaps at or near the Shell Ring? There is some evidence to support that possibility. With Herb Boyett, a friend and specialist in Native American and Spanish mission history, I visited the St. Catherines mission by water in 1996 during a long weekend on the water. The trip including explorations of the adjoining waterways in Liberty and Bryan counties, including St. Catherines and Ossabaw islands.

* * *

Fort King George was established in 1721 by South Carolina Rangers under Col. John Barnwell, it was the first English outpost in Georgia, preceding the actual founding of the colony a dozen years later. Since the late 1960s it has been a state historic site, with a replica cypress blockhouse erected in 1989, followed by assorted other buildings. However, in the 1950s, when I attended the Darien public school, there was nothing at Fort King Georgia except a marble monument signifying the site, and the small markers of the graves of several of the English soldiers who died at the fort in the 1720s. As second and third graders, and later in our Georgia history classes in the seventh grade, our teachers would often lead our classes on walks down the sandy dirt road from the schoolhouse to Lower Bluff to look around.

Some of my fellow students were disappointed not to see an actual "fort" at Fort King George. But I knew better—from being regaled by the stories of the fort by McIntosh historian Bessie Lewis and my repeated reading of coastal historian Margaret Davis Cate's *Early Days of Coastal Georgia* in the mid-to-late 1950s, I realized then that this was a special place of historic significance amid the old moss-draped live oaks, the cedar trees and the views across the Darien River marshes and Altamaha delta. Later, I made approaches to the fort site by water in my boat. This offers a unique perspective, particularly after the reconstruction of the fort's cypress blockhouse and other buildings starting in 1989. The attractive map on the preceding page was prepared in 1955 (at the time I was making those first school walks to the site with classmates) on his letterpress by William G. Haynes of the Ashantilly Press. It is very accurate and is based on the definitive research of the fort's 1721-27 existence by Bessie Lewis and Haynes himself.

* * *

Butler's Island is a unique place. By the first decade of the nineteenth century McIntosh County had become an economy based on rice and cotton agriculture. Thomas Spalding at Sapelo Island (cotton and sugar cane), and Major Pierce Butler at Butler's Island (rice) were the leading agrarians in the county, and the largest slave holders. The Butler's Island rice plantation was at peak productivity in the late 1830s and early 1840s, about the time of the visit of Frances Anne Kemble and her husband Pierce Mease Butler from their Philadelphia home on an inspection tour of the family's Georgia plantations. Butler's Island was the largest producer of rice among the numerous tracts in the Altamaha delta. The Butlers also produced secondary rotation crops—cotton and sugar cane—before concentrating exclusively on rice, which by 1845, had become the primary cash crop produced in the Georgia and South Carolina low country. There were four separate slave settlements, designated as Nos. 1, 2, 3 and 4, various landings on the surrounding tidal rivers, and the plantation complex where were located the overseer's house, the rice mill and the main dock. In her *Journal of a Residence on a Georgian Plantation in 1838-1839*, published in 1863, Fanny Kemble provides valuable details about the physical layout and infrastructure of Butler's Island. I have relied on her accounts for much of my understanding of antebellum Butler's Island and have cited the *Journal* extensively in my books. Revealing too, is the comprehensive

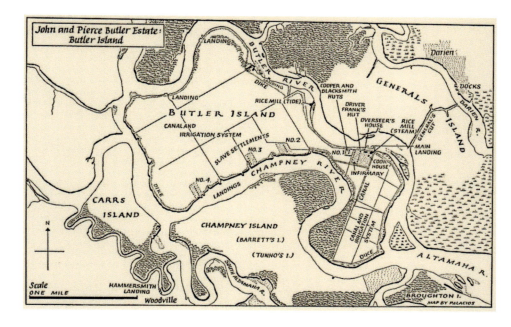

archaeological field work done by Theresa Singleton in 1979, also cited in my work. One of my mentors, Malcolm Bell, Jr., wrote by far the most vivid and sweeping account of the Butlers and their tidewater plantations in his study, *Major Butler's Legacy.* Now, almost two hundred years after Kemble's visit, oe can still walk the levees and embankments along the Butler and Champney rivers and have a good feel for the rice plantation and the conditions under which the enslaved people there must have endured from both an environmental standpoint as well as that of the rigid discipline as enforced by two long-term overseers, Roswell King, followed by his son, Roswell King Jr., from 1802 to 1854. Pursuant to my research for various books about McIntosh County, Butler's Island, and the journal of Roswell King, Jr., I often walked the grounds and levees of the island—the old brick rice mill stack is the most visible testimony of rice culture on the coast—and by boat along the adjoining Butler and Champney rivers. I also trod the sites of the settlements of enslaved people. Very little remains except some scattered brick and tabby fragments attesting to human occupation, but the sensation of experiencing the "presence" of real and tangible history is evident when visiting Butler's Island. It is unpopulated, remote and completely natural in parts of it, adding to the pervasive sense of history, culture—and human suffering—from hundreds of years ago.

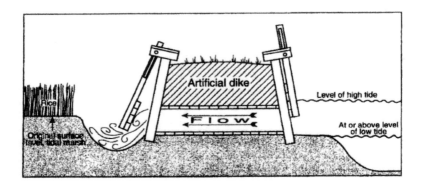

Artificial dike

Level of high tide

At or above level of low tide

Rice

Original surface level, tidal marsh

FLOW

This sketch shows a typical arrangement for flooding and draining rice fields. Fresh water from upriver is allowed into the field through tidegates on the outgoing tide. The gates, (or trunks) are then closed to prevent the unwanted inflow of mostly salt water on the incoming tide on the next six-hour tidal cycle. Rice was planted in staggered cycles in the spring with four floodings and drainings of fields, or squares, during the growing cycle. When fields were drained, weeds and other intrusive growths harmful to the delicate rice shoots were removed by the workers, usually females and older children. Harvesting began in late August followed by threshing and pounding. Only the larger plantations had their own pounding machinery at steam mills, Butler's Island being the prime example. Pounding mills were prohibitively expensive for most. In boat travels along the various streams of the Altamaha delta, I have observed much evidence of the remains of rotting tidegates, as well as what is left of levees and embankments along the river edges—reflections of the era of nineteenth century rice production during which McIntosh County ranked as one of the wealthiest in Georgia.

* * *

Broughton Island plantation was the easternmost of the McIntosh County rice tracts in the Altamaha basin. It was planted by the Brailsford, Troup and Bryan families in the antebellum period with consistently high yields of production. My study of the 1869 U.S. Coast Survey topographic of the lower Altamaha region divulged the main irrigation canals bisecting the fields at Broughton, and the plantation complex with slave dwellings and threshing mill on the lower side of the canal, the plantation house on the opposite side and foot-walks providing access both ways. In my boating explorations I have traversed the tidal main canal and viewed the brick remains of the mill. The canal is now thickly covered by the undergrowth of numerous types of vegetation but is still passable for a good distance from the river. This section is wild, mysterious and even somewhat forbidding, especially with the occasional sightings of alligators and water moccasins. I wouldn't venture there at night.

* * *

There were many antebellum upland farm tracts, large and small, on the eastern McIntosh tidewater, roughly paralleling the Cow Horn Road (present highway 99) from Darien to Sapelo Bridge (present-day Eulonia). These plantations produced both sea island and short staple cotton as their primary cash crops. Some of these tracts were owned by families whose ancestors continue to have a presence in McIntosh County. There were several plantations in the area of the present-day Meridian and Hudson communities, including those of John Hudson, John Lafong at Patterson Island, and the Meadows, the cotton tract of Horace Jesse Harrison, and later Charles H. Hopkins. The tidal stream abutting these tracts is Atwood Creek, which flows in to the south section of the sizeable Manchester plantation lands of James Nephew, and which a portion of later became Shell Bluff-Valona. This area was decimated by the severe hurricane which struck the coast in September 1824, the worst storm on record ever to directly impact McIntosh County. My books, *Early Days on the Georgia Tidewater* and *Low Country Historian* provide detailed contemporary accounts of this terrible storm and its effects on local citizens. On a more personal note, for ten years, from 1985 to 1995, my family and I resided in a home we built on Kittles Island, the lower section of the marsh island situated on the map between the Meadows and the Hudson plantation. I have visited virtually all of the Cow Horn Road tracts from the Ridge to the Forest, the latter being the Wylly family plantation on the upper Sapelo River near present Eulonia. In between, from south to north, are the Thicket, where the tabby ruins of William Carnochan's sugar mill and rum distillery are still very much in evidence—this was an enterprising business that thrived for eight years from 1816 until being destroyed in the 1824 hurricane; Woodville and Brighton (Smith and Gignilliat families), Hudson, Patterson Island, the Meadows, Manchester, Cedar Point (Henry S. Atwood), and Baisden's Bluff and Belleville (the Hopkins family holdings) that encompassed a large area on either side of the present Crescent community and extending northward along the Crescent (South Sapelo) River to the Sapelo River. There are so many memories and personal associations from this section of the eastern McIntosh County tidewater. There are such locales as Hudson Creek and landing, the Sapelo Island ferry dock built by Howard Coffin in the 1920s from which I commuted to my work on Sapelo on the state-operated ferry vessels, nearby Kittles Island opposite Patterson Island on Atwood Creek, the Meadows north of Kittles, and the Kittles shrimp docks on the lower end of Valona. There were frequent boat outings on these waters in my adolescence, particularly in friendships with the children of Peter Kittles and his brother George Kittles who had several shrimp boats at the dock, with their homes close by. As children, we often fished at the dock at Patterson Island. I also remember the charred remains of the hull of the shrimp boat *Miss Meta* in Atwood Creek in the marsh and mudflats just south of Patterson. It caught fire and burned to the waterline in the summer of 1960 and was beached there by Captain Jiggs Redding. At the confluence of Atwood and Hudson creeks at the head of Doboy Sound, we often followed the Carnigan River to one of its tributaries, Crum Creek, to access the Thicket and its tabby ruins.

* * *

In the upper part of McIntosh County there were extensive agricultural operations on large and small farm tracts along the Sapelo and South Newport rivers throughout the antebellum period, and during the Civil War. U.S. Coast Survey charts and topographical maps for Sapelo Sound in the 1850s show part of lower Bruro Neck under cultivation. One tract is shown as "Brailsford," the plantation of William Brailsford at *Sutherland's Bluff*. The maps reveal slave dwellings and fields under cultivation. There is a dirt road shown leading north to "Cooke," that being the plantation of William Cooke called Shellman—and being on the site of what years later became the waterfront community of *Shellman Bluff*. At the south end of the road is the landing on the Sapelo River by which water access was made to the north end of Creighton Island, another of Cooke's cotton tracts. Nearby is Fourmile Island, a marsh island fronting on Sapelo and Bruro rivers. In the 1950s and 1960s Sutherland's Bluff was a maritime forest of pine, oak and other hardwoods, and was one of the most remote parts of the county. A sandy road led from Shellman Bluff led down to the bluff on the Sapelo River. As a 13-year-old Boy Scout we enjoyed several weekend camping trips to Sutherland's Bluff, often feeling we had gone to the ends of the earth because of the remoteness of the site with no evidence of anything resembling civilization. Later, in the

1990s, the Bluff, and neighboring Travelers Rest, became an upscale residential development, with a golf course and clubhouse.

* * *

In 1785-86 British Loyalist Francis Levett began experimenting with the cultivation of long-staple sea island cotton at his *Julianton plantation* on the lower end of Harris Neck—then a part of Liberty County since McIntosh was not created from Liberty until 1793. Along with James Spalding of St. Simons Island, Richard Leake at Jekyll Island and several planters in Chatham County, Levett was in the first group to experiment with sea island cotton in the United States in the years immediately after the Reolution. Levett was a large slave owner and his plantation complex was quite extensive. Old surveys depict cultivated fields, wooded areas, slave dwellings, a main house and various outbuildings situated near the landing on the Julianton River. Levett named his plantation Julianton for his mother, Juliana Levett. Pursuant to my ongoing research for *Early Days on the Georgia Tidewater*, I made several boat excursions across Sapelo Sound to the Julianton River, thence to the site of Julianton itself to view the landscape of the former plantation and its waterfront. Mr. Gene Slivka had established his private home in the mid-1980s on about the same footprint as that of Francis Levett. Levett died at Julianton in 1802 as a relatively young man at the age of forty-eight and is buried on the site. Julianton continued to be managed as a cotton plantation by Levett's descendants until 1861. It was later acquired in 1917 by Elisha M. Thorpe, another important figure in the history of McIntosh County. I have always been fascinated by the story of Julianton and Francis Levett. In exploring this section of the Julianton River by boat I have always been struck by the feeling of quietness and solitude evoked by the ecology and history on this end of the Neck, even though the bustling recreational fishing community of Shellman Bluff is but a short distance away. As of 2023 this lower section of Harris Neck remains undeveloped.

* * *

Ecologically, *Harris Neck* is a marsh island as it is surrounded by salt marsh, and tidal streams, with the upper end (the Wildlife Refuge) linked to the mainland by a short causeway. The South Newport River flows across the upper end of the Neck; the Barbour Island River runs along much of the east side with access at Gould's Landing, and Harris Neck Creek and the Julianton River flow along the west side of Harris Neck. In the plantation era, Gould's Landing provided water access to the smaller marsh islands—Barbour Island and Wahoo Island—which served as small auxiliary cotton tracts to the larger plantations on Harris Neck. During the antebellum era there were several plantations on Harris Neck devoted to the production of sea island and short staple cotton as their primary cash crops. On the upper part of Harris Neck was the Peru plantation of Jonathan Thomas (d. ca. 1849) and his son, John Abbott Thomas (d. 1859), from ca. 1816 to 1861. Adjoining tracts were those of John Harris (d. 1839) and his widow Margaret Harris. Nearby were the farm tract of William John King, and Delta, the tract of succeeding members of the Delegal family. Across Harris Neck Creek to the west was Belvedere, a cotton tract owned in succession by James Gignilliat, Edward Postell, Jonathan Thomas and Margaret Harris. Delta extended down the Neck, abutting the Harris and King plantations on the north and east, and Julianton to the south. Across Harris Neck Creek, is the Dunham tract of Margaret Harris. Much of the land now comprises the Harris Neck Wildlife Refuge. Margaret Harris died in 1866 and her substantial properties, including the Harris plantation, Belvedere and Dunham, were sold out of the family. Gould's Landing is part of the wildlife refuge and is the site of the antebellum Bahama plantation of Thomas K. Gould. Nearby is the Gould Cemetery, a post-Civil War burial ground begun by the freedmen of Harris Neck and still in use today. Several artesian wells are south of the Refuge where the Harris and King plantations would have been located on the Barbour Island River, the tidal stream on the east. In the 1920s, Gould's Landing was the site of an oyster cannery developed by Augustus Oemler of Savannah and St. Catherines Island. A 1940s map shows a "Rotating Light" on the sandy road on the south end of present refuge. It is a vestige of the World War II Harris Neck Army Air Field, which encompassed the area of what is now the wildlife refuge. These were the lands of plantations and the later Geechee community of freedmen and their descendants. Many had bought upper Harris Neck land from the descendants of their former owners in the period after the Civil War. Their land was condemned in 1941 and taken by the federal government to build the air field where there once many structures, most of which have disappeared, and concrete runways, some of which are still in place, though largely overgrown with vegetation. Many are the times I have explored this entire section of the Neck, investigating the cemetery, the former airfield, and Gould's Landing where a small concrete bridge once spanned the Barbour Island

River. I took photographs and made notes on these and other parts of upper Harris Neck pursuant to my research on the history of this intriguing area. It was easy for me to see in my mind's eye an era when fields were under cultivation in cotton, boats loading farm staples for shipment at Gould's Landing and at Peru plantation's Thomas Landing, images of wood-frame slave dwellings, and the simple, unostentatious wood-frame plantation houses on each of the separate farm tracts. Harris Neck, partly due I believe to its remoteness and virtual isolation from the rest of McIntosh County, is one of the most interesting areas of coastal Georgia, be it historical or ecological. I have devoted extensive coverage of the history of the area in my books, most recently in *Low Country Historian,* which has my most complete data and up-to-date research.

* * *

Two-and-a-quarter miles west of Shellman Bluff is the *White Chimney River.* On either side of this tidal stream there were antebellum farm tracts. One was Cannon's Bluff, scene of agricultural activities by the Cannon family in the antebellum period and during the Civil War. Across the White Chimney and its marshes was the small plantation of Margery Forbes and her children, she being the widow of John Forbes, the overseer of Daniel H. Brailsford's Sutherland's Bluff plantation. In 1833, Forbes murdered the young Brailsford at Sapelo Bridge in one of the most unusual cases in McIntosh County history (for the particulars see any of my books about the county). The modern residential community of White Chimney is on the lower end of Bruro Neck. To its east is Travelers Rest, once a farm tract, now a residential area, and beyond that is Sutherland's Bluff. An 1882 county map shows a wooden bridge over the White Chimney River where the present bridge is now on the way to Shellman Bluff. Small boats under sail once came up as far the bridge to take on cargoes of farm staples and turpentine before and after the war. Besides the Cannon and Forbes families, other agricultural tracts in this section were held by William Hope and Francis Durant. There are three very interesting burial grounds in this section: The Point Cemetery is within the present White Chimney community just south of the Shellman Bluff Road on land that was formerly the Forbes family land. Here are buried descendants of slaves from this part of McIntosh County, some with the surnames of their former owners such as Spaulding, Dunham and Delegal; Cannon-Forbes Cemetery, a small plot on the north side of the Shellman Road; and the Mints Cemetery on the opposite side of the White Chimney River not far from the bridge and south of the Shellman road.

* * *

Creighton Narrows (Scott Creek) on the southeast side of Creighton Island was and is a frequently used passage linking areas such as Cedar Point and Valona with Sapelo Sound, one I have traversed countless times. The Narrows is fringed on either side by small hammocks that have grown with vegetation where dredge spoil was deposited in the 1940s and 1950s. In 1913, the Corps of Engineers completed the construction of a cut through the marsh of Scott Creek to re-route the Atlantic Intracoastal Waterway from Sapelo Sound to Doboy Sound via Front River. Creighton Narrows, as it was called, met the Dividings at Mud River, then the route carried through Old Teakettle Creek to Doboy Sound. This bypassed the old route through the shallow Mud River which connected to Doboy through New Teakettle Creek on the west side of Sapelo Island. As adolescents in the 50s and 60s we often camped on the hammocks in the summer. I have a personal attachment to this area for, as a teenager, my friends and I built a campsite on the tiny hammock marked "New Creighton" where Creighton Narrows meets the Dividings. We sat long into the night by a campfire eating canned beans and saltine crackers and watching the occasional freight barge travel past along the intracoastal waterway. Nowadays from my home at Cedar Point I can look out my window and see this section of the Narrows, with Mud River and the Dividings, and view shrimp boats, recreational craft and the occasional barge transiting though. The Dividings is formed by the confluence of several tidal waterways: Crescent River (South Sapelo River on some charts and maps), Creighton Narrows, Mud River, Shellbluff Creek leading to Valona, and Old Teakettle Creek. The currents and tidal dynamics in this part of the Intracoastal Waterway are often contradictory, depending on wind direction. This is my favorite part of all the McIntosh County waterways as it links Cedar Point and Valona, places I have frequented all my life. Nearby, just south, is Old Teakettle Creek linking the Dividings to a merger with New Teakettle, thence into Doboy Sound. From the water along this route can be seen Patterson Island on Atwood Creek, and a portion of Little Sapelo Island. Old Teakettle to Doboy Sound and Creighton Narrows to Sapelo Sound were like a "thoroughfare" for my adolescent boating explorations. Later, as an adult, I made countless crossings of upper and lower Doboy Sound from Hudson Creek dock to Marsh Landing dock, passing by the confluence of Old Teakettle while commuting to work on Sapelo Island on the state ferry vessel, or occasionally in an open boat.

* * *

Various USGS topographic maps from the 1950s to the 1990s depict *Creighton Island*, discussed earlier in this chapter as the venue of many of my early boat explorations. This privately-owned 1,000-acre back-barrier island accessible only by water is unpopulated. There are several sandy roads, more like trails, in the middle of the island and on its north end where there are tabby ruins of slave dwellings—testament to Creighton's being an antebellum cotton tract. I have traversed the road several times. It runs from the north end and terminates near the cattle landing on the south end of the island. In childhood I enjoyed pleasant visits by boat to Creighton as the guest of Mr. Will Williams of Baisden's Bluff, one of the Williams brothers who co-owned the island. I well recall the cattle and timber landings on the south end—one on the Crescent River, and the other on the southeast side on Creighton Narrows-Front River. Several of my boat travels have entailed circumnavigations of the island. Parts of this trip require an extra high spring tide. Starting at Hazzard's ballast hammock on the Front River, I have utilized Ridge River Mouth to access the northeastern tip of Creighton where an occasional wild cow can be seen grazing in the high marsh by the creek. On spring tide, I have gone across the north end of Creighton to Back River, thence to July Cut and into Crescent River on the southwest side of the island down to its junction with Creighton Narrows near the Dividings. Creighton is one of the true treasures of the Georgia coast, still privately owned and thus unspoiled, undeveloped, and properly conserved. Long may it remain so.

* * *

Hazzard's ballast hammock, east of Creighton at the north end of Front River at its juncture with Sapelo Sound, is a place that holds many pleasant memories. Over a hundred years ago ships, some sail and some steel, steam-powered vessels, berthed here loading timber. Early 1900s images reveal very little vegetation on Hazzard's. The scrub oak, red cedar and sabal palm, along with a thick understory of wax myrtle and marsh elder, have developed in the century since the timber era (see the photo on page 28). William Hazzard's store provided artesian well water, and groceries to shipping frequenting Sapelo Sound. In the early 1900s it even had a telephone connecting the hammock to the mainland. There are three small hammocks in the Hazzard's group. The largest has the greatest deposits of ballast rock still to be seen along the shore of Front River. A creek, Ridge River Mouth, runs from the hammocks up to the northeast point of Creighton Island, which in the timber era had a sizeable African American population largely employed by the local timber concerns as stevedores and watermen.

I have visited Hazzard's ballast hammock and explored the other Front River hammocks many times throughout my life in McIntosh County. As a child we frequently fished and crabbed at Hazzard's and enjoyed the pure, cold water from the free-flowing artesian well there amid the ballast rocks. We scavenged for bottles from Europe and ceramic sherds scattered amid the ballast stone, rarely cognizant of the significance of these rare little pieces of our local maritime history at the time. Years later, as an adult exploring Hazzard's there was nary a bottle or vial to be found. The hammock had been picked clean by artifact seekers. But the European ballast rock is still there.

* * *

Transiting *Sapelo Sound* east toward the open Atlantic enabled me on a number of occasions to visit remote and unpopulated *Blackbeard Island,* a beautiful national wildlife refuge and the scene of some of McIntosh County's most interesting history. Here were active live oak timbering operations by the U.S. Navy to build wooden warships in northern shipyards in the first decades of the nineteenth century. From 1880-1910 the federal Blackbeard Island quarantine station inspected arriving ships on the coast for possible outbreaks of the deadly yellow fever and other tropical diseases. From the refuge dock on Blackbeard Creek one can walk a short distance to the beach on the opposite side of the island. Further north is Flag Pond, a brackish fresh water quasi-reservoir populated by alligators and snakes. Nearby, and overlooking Sapelo Sound, is the brick crematory, the only vestige that survives from the quarantine period. My research has failed to divulge any use of the crematory to dispose of the bodies of yellow fever victims, not surprising since it was not constructed by the Marine Hospital Service until 1905. By then, vaccines had been developed to all but eliminate the yellow fever scourge which had exacted terrible epidemics and loss of life in coastal cities such as Charleston, Savannah and New Orleans. I have often transited Blackbeard Creek and its marshes that separate Blackbeard from Sapelo Island. The lower end of Blackbeard Creek enters the Atlantic Ocean at Cabretta Inlet. This is a wild and pristine area of natural beauty accentuated by the transition from salt marsh zones, to barrier island beaches, to the ocean itself. For the adventurous, Cabretta Creek, separating Cabretta Island from Sapelo, may be traversed for a couple of miles from the Inlet, a quiet, pleasant journey highlighted by the observation of numerous species of waterfowl and marine life, and the always-invigorating aromas of the marsh mixed with those of the nearby sea wafted across Cabretta Island by the offshore breezes.

* * *

As a Georgia Department of Natural Resources employee supervising the *Sapelo Island* National Estuarine Research Reserve for better than two decades, I had ample opportunity to explore every part of Sapelo, both by land and by water. The remote unpopulated north end of Sapelo is especially interesting. In that section is High Point overlooking Sapelo Sound. Slightly south and east of High Point via a connecting causeway through the marsh is the neck of land known as Dumoussay Field, named for one of 1790s French investors who owned the tract. (The story of the short-lived French consortium's experience on Sapelo, 1789-1795, is a fascinating one and receives full ample attention in my books—the most complete account is in *Sapelo: People and Place on a Georgia Sea Island*). Southeast of Dumoussay is Bourbon Field, one of the Thomas Spalding cotton tracts. The High Point road which runs along the west side of Sapelo north to south, has historically significant areas, including the Native American Shell Ring, an oyster shell ceremonial mound dating back about 3,800 years; the tabby ruins of the Chocolate plantation tract overlooking Mud River toward the mainland—there are tabby remains dating the period 1815-1837 of the barn, several slave dwellings and a cotton storage house. A little further south are such long-abandoned locales as Belle Marsh, Moses Hammock and Lumber Landing, both on the Duplin River, the old Kenan Field cotton tract on the Duplin, and the remnants of Hanging Bull, once the slave settlement for the Kenan-Spalding plantation. In my years of employment with Georgia DNR, I spent countless hours exploring these areas of the island in relation to my interest in the history of the North End, and my desire to frequently obtain a first-hand "feel" for the parts of Sapelo that I was researching and writing about. All of this section is part of the Reynolds Wildlife Management Area; it is remote, isolated and unpopulated. The hardwood maritime forests, marshes and the grassy savannas here evoke a long-ago era of agriculture, and the vestiges of long-gone freedmen settlements such as Raccoon Bluff, once the most populous Geechee settlement on Sapelo.

* * *

Some of my most rewarding boating forays were in and around *Doboy Sound*, a tidal embayment that meets the Atlantic Ocean on the south end of Sapelo Island. This was a historic anchorage for timber ships 150 years ago, arriving from Europe to load the raw timber and processed lumber from the saw mills at Darien and Doboy Island. There have always been navigational hazards associated with the entrance to Doboy Sound. These were long a detriment to the advancement of Darien as a major seaport—involving sandbars, shoals and breakers, including Pelican Spit and Chimney Spit just offshore, with a narrow channel into the anchorage between the Sapelo Island lighthouse and the range beacon on Wolf Island across the Sound from Sapelo lighthouse and the lower end of Nanny Goat Beach. I can personally attest to the shallowness of the Sound's entrance at the lower tides near the north end of Wolf Island, having grounded my boat on barely submerged sandbars at times.

* * *

Sapelo lighthouse is on South End Creek and its marshes overlooking Doboy Sound. There were actually two lighthouses on the marsh hammock, the first being the still-standing 80-foot brick tower built in 1820, and the second a 125-foot steel tower built a few yards north after the 1898 hurricane undermined the foundations of the brick light. Until the R.J. Reynolds ownership of Sapelo Island starting in 1934, the only convenient way to access the lighthouse from the main island was via South End Creek, or from Doboy Sound into which the creek entered near the lighthouse island. In 1950, Reynolds had a causeway built from the beach road to the lighthouse to enable vehicle access to the long-abandoned brick tower. The second Sapelo light station was deactivated in 1933 due to the almost total lack of shipping entering Doboy Sound with the end of Darien's timber prosperity. The disassembled tower was transported by barge to Lake Michigan and rebuilt. I have walked the sites of both the 1820 and 1905 lighthouses many times. Of course, the brick tower still stands overlooking Doboy Sound, being restored and re-lit as a navigation aid in 1998 during my tenure as manager of the Sapelo Island Research Reserve. All that remains of the 1905 light are the concrete foot pads for the tower and the brick oil house used to store the kerosene that fueled the lamp. Followers of my research know that I have always been fascinated by the history of the two Sapelo lighthouses, and they feature prominently in my books about Sapelo and McIntosh County. The lights truly evoke the important, and colorful, maritime legacy of the county with its flashing beacon long a comforting reference mark for timber ships, fishing craft and offshore craft.

As manager of the Estuarine Research Reserve on Sapelo perhaps the most satisfying project in which I was involved was the restoration of the brick lighthouse. The light was re-lit with appropriate ceremony in September 1998. Many are the times I have climbed the rebuilt wooden steps to the top and marveled at the expansive views afforded over the sea, Doboy Sound and its marshes, and Sapelo's uplands and the mainland beyond. To me, the light affords the best views of anywhere in McIntosh County. The 1868 Coast Survey topographic map of "Doboy Sound & Vicinity" denotes the lower end of Sapelo and the lighthouse tract. There was a plank walk-causeway through the marsh along the creek linking the South End to the lighthouse island. I have searched high and low for evidence of this plank-walk but not a trace of it remains.

* * *

Sapelo South End has changed because of the dynamics of current flow from the offshore Gulf Stream, along with wind, tropical storms and the natural accretion of sand from north to south, a phenomenon prevalent on the Georgia and lower South Carolina barrier islands. Except for the changing shoreline and the sand accretion on the lower end of Nanny Goat Beach, the topographic features of this part of Sapelo are about the same today (2023) as they were on a 1954 topo map of the Doboy Sound area that I have studied many times. A telephone line from the mainland to the R.J. Reynolds house is shown. At the head of South End Creek, labeled "Sapelo," are the buildings of the University of Georgia Marine Institute, created only the year before the map was done (the structures were originally built by Reynolds in the mid-1930s). Also shown is H.E. Coffin's 1920s "water garden" opposite the Marine Institute. This part of the South End is little changed in the present day, except for the modernizations and improvements to the research buildings of UGAMI. At Nanny Goat beach the map delineates wood pilings emplaced in the shallows in the 1940s, ostensibly for the installation of shark nets when necessary. The beach dunes have considerably altered in the last seventy years. Now there are two distinct lines of dunes. Dean Creek partly parallels the lighthouse

119

road from the beach causeway to the lighthouse, built by Reynolds had had it built. The road (trail) is still in place leading to the restored lighthouse, its nearby range beacon, and the remains of an 1898 gun emplacement originally built by Confederate units in 1862 and rebuilt with concrete by the U.S. Army during the Spanish-American War.

* * *

Doboy Island is mostly a marsh tract with only a hundred acres or so of high ground on which were once located a saw mill, store and housing for mill workers, mostly freedmen, during the Reconstruction period and beyond. My boat trips occasionally took me into Back River which flows along *Commodore Island* and the south part of Doboy Island. Nearby, the waters of Doboy Sound are often quite rough. with a heavy chop depending on wind direction and tidal flow. An ebbing tide down the Sound toward the open sea, going against a southeasterly wind, which is often prevalent, makes for challenging conditions for the small boat enthusiast. I have often experienced these conditions in my boats over the years, occasionally encountering rough water that necessitated temporary sanctuary in a convenient marsh bordering the Sound. In my years employed on Sapelo when daily commutes on the ferry from the Hudson Creek dock to Marsh Landing on the Duplin, the Sound was often quite bumpy, even for a vessel of that size.

In the postbellum period from 1865 to about 1890, sailing vessels from the United Kingdom, Germany and Scandinavia would, in season, fill Doboy Sound loading cargoes of raw timber and processed lumber from the local mills. Prior to taking on lumber, the foreign ships unloaded ballast rock in the marshes around Doboy Island, still visible along North River and *Rock Island.* There was a saw mill on Cane Creek, across North River from Doboy Island. To me, it is one of the most interesting places on the McIntosh County tidewater. I have walked along the shell trail there amid the low scrub growth and cedar trees and found rusting pieces of machinery attesting to the activity associated with the timber prosperity of that long-ago era. This was a time when Darien stood unchallenged as the leading exporter of yellow pine timber on the Atlantic coast. A.C. McKinley's 1870s journal noted large numbers of ships around Doboy depositing ballast and taking on timber and lumber. Near Doboy is Queens Island, mostly marsh and beach, which served as a quarantine for sailors before and after the Civil War.

Doboy Island is one of the most interesting places in McIntosh County, and not just because of its unusual name. The island gets its name from Doboy Sound of course, which itself is an Anglicization of the inlet designated on sixteenth century French maps in recognition of Johan Duboys, or Dubois, a French navigator who investigated this part of coast in the 1660s. The 1954 USGS topo map shows the marshes and small upland area of Doboy Island with the largely marsh island of Commodore and its nine tiny hammocks along the Back River. The Back River was a preferred ship anchorage for vessels in the 1870s and 1880s because of the shelter afforded by Commodore Island. The small hammocks with their attendant ballast deposits are in evidence today. These were collectively known in the timber era as "Cane Creek" but now more familiarly known as Rock Island—obviously so named for the ballast stone in the marshes along the river. On one of the hammocks was a saw mill and timber loading docks. Across North River on Doboy were more extensive docks for the ships. I have enjoyed many interesting visits exploring Doboy, Commodore and Rock islands over the years in my waterway forays. The private owners of these tracts have always been gracious in accommodating my visits in pursuit of historical research, as well as my occasionally leading historical tours of Doboy for groups from other parts of Georgia participating in the annual Weekend for Wildlife event hosted by the Department of Natural Resources.

* * *

Contiguous to Doboy Sound is the lower end of *Old Teakettle Creek* on the east side of which is Little Sapelo Island, which itself fronts on the lower Duplin River near the Sapelo Island ferry dock. Further up the Sound is the confluence of three tidal streams—Carnigan River, Hudson Creek and Atwood Creek. This has always been an interesting area to me and one of frequent water and land investigations. My family built a home on nearby Kittles Island on Atwood Creek in 1990, and the community dock there enabled me to have convenient access to the whole section by water. From that point my children and I made boat excursions down Doboy Sound to swim in the waters at Nanny Goat beach across the from the lighthouse, to Doboy and Commodore, excursions to Blackbeard, and enjoyable water trips to Darien via North River, Blue and Hall landing and Black Island Creek. Those were special times in the 1990s. Also in this section are the waterways and islands between the Ridge and Doboy Island, the largest being Hird and Black islands. On the mainland is the *Ridge* community, about three miles

121

northeast of Darien on either side of the Cow Horn Road. There was once a plank walk-causeway through the marsh connecting the Ridge to Blue and Hall, at which was a saw mill before the Civil War. Blue and Hall was typically the departure point for those traveling by water to Doboy Sound and points beyond. It was frequently used by the bar pilots who resided on the Ridge to get to their pilot vessels to guide the timber ships into and out of the harbor. One could get a boat from Blue and Hall across the North River to another plank walk through the marsh to access *Union Island* where the Hiltons and Lachlisons operated a saw mill after the war. Before and after the war, Union Island was more familiarly known as Pumpkin Hammock and was marked as such on many maps. Due south of Union Island is the upper part of *Black Island,* which is a short distance north and east of Lower Bluff and the Darien River. Following North River eastward one comes to *Hird Island* on the upper end of which was a saw mill. North of Hird Island is Buzzard Roost Creek and Buzzard Roost Island, a small marsh hammock. In my adolescence, our Boy Scout troop spent a weekend camping on Hird Island, being transported there from Valona on Fred Todd's shrimp boat. Later in life, I have boated on these waters between Blue and Hall and Doboy Sound, enjoying the ecology and the natural beauty of the area while reflecting on its interesting history.

* * *

The area between Valona and the Ridge (Ridgeville) includes Hudson, Meridian, Carneghan and the Thicket, the latter being the present, and misnamed, Tolomato residential community. Access is by state highway 99, known historically as the Cow Horn Road. A mile north of Meridian is the Hudson community, with a county leading half a mile east to Meridian Landing on Hudson Creek. Much is the section encompassed the antebellum plantation lands of John Hudson. Nearby is *Kittles Island,* a property owned in the early 1900s by oyster fisherman William A. Kittles whose docks and cannery were a short distance further up Atwood Creek on the south end of Valona. South of Meridian is the neck of land called Pease Point, the northern extension of the *Thicket,* with water access from Hudson Creek. Much of this land was once held by Theodore P. Pease who came to McIntosh County in the early 1840s from Connecticut. He and his family lived at the Thicket near the old sugar mill ruins before, during and after the Civil War. The tabby sugar mill and rum distillery at the Thicket built in 1816 by William Carnochan are accessible by land from highway 99 and by water from Crum Creek, a tributary of the Carnigan River further east. The facility was heavily damaged in the September 1824 hurricane which ravaged this section of coastal Georgia and was never rebuilt. In my adolescence our Boy Scout troop camped at the Thicket on the banks of Crum Creek. This was long before the residential development of the section.

* * *

I have made many auto explorations into the remote, sparsely populated western sections of McIntosh County, always in search of the interesting history of the area. I define this area as that which is west of Interstate 95. The great majority of the county's population has always been east of present 95, nearer to the tidal waterways. This was expedient in the early days of the county, for the plantations were usually contiguous to water and getting one's agricultural commodities to the bigger markets was, from necessity, by boats and small sailing vessels. *Townsend*, established as a railroad whistle stop in the early 1890s, is the only settlement of substance in western McIntosh. There are other, smaller communities such as Jones in the northwest corner of the county, and Cox in the lower southwest section in the sand hills not far from the Altamaha River. In my travels about this section viewing such sites as the concrete silos used to maintain large herds of free-ranging cattle in an unsuccessful venture by the Georgia Land & Livestock Company in the 1920s, or remnants of the railroad, abandoned since 1985, I was always struck by how the history, culture, and especially the ecology of the western part of the county is so vastly different from the tidal areas. The area along the Steel Bridge Road linking Townsend and Cox is exceedingly remote and is essentially unpopulated as far as the eye can see. The same may be said for the dirt road between Townsend and Jones going in the opposite direction, north. The landscape along these rarely-traveled roads (except for hunters and timber cutters) exemplifies the western McIntosh pine flatwoods—pine, oak and saw palmetto understories, and the scene of timbering, naval stores and turpentine distilleries, along with the railroad that made these early twentieth century activities possible for the hardy families who undertook them. Several small railroad settlements have long since disappeared. One of them was *Warsaw*, between Townsend and Jones and on the spur track of the Seaboard Airline R.R. Warsaw was the county's most active lumber producer in the 1920s and early 1930s. A settlement of mill workers and their families developed near the railroad and timber cut in the area was brought in to

Warsaw to be processed into lumber. There was a spur from the Seaboard to the saw mill, with extensive lumber sheds and dwellings nearby. Nothing of Warsaw remains except the brick vault of the Warsaw Lumber Company office. A picture of it will be seen in the next chapter of this book.

Between Warsaw and Jones was the little settlement of *Brickstone* (pronounced *Brix-tun*). Near the Seaboard tracks were a brick-making plant and workers' housing. It operated from 1905 to 1918. When the brick plant ended operations the few people that were left moved away. Not long after, in 1934, the Warsaw saw mill burned and the owners elected not to rebuild it. The mill community gradually disappeared as people left, except for a few who remained in the area to produce turpentine. Warsaw and Brickstone were both non-existent by World War II. Halfway between Warsaw and the Atlantic Coastal Highway (US 17) is *Young's Island,* another remote settlement in the center of McIntosh County, populated by several generations of the Young family. Some Young's Island residents made their way along a logging trail to work in the Warsaw saw mill. I have visited Young's Island and its church and cemetery. It is indeed remote and, like Warsaw, far off the beaten track.

* * *

Downtown *Darien,* as noted in my memoir in the first chapter, was a special place for me in the 1950s and 1960s. Long have I studied the 1954 USGS topographic map of Darien, which accurately shows the location and configuration of every building in all of the town at the time. The population in the 1950s was around 1,400, about the same as it was during the prosperous timber era a half century earlier. The 1954 map is valuable because it depicts Darien before the widening of US 17 through town in the early 1970s. That project completely altered the layout of Walton Street and eliminated some buildings, including several businesses that had been a bedrock of the community for years, such as Archie's Darien Grill, Mr. Wilkins' gas station and the B & B Variety Store. The 1954 map also delineates in detail the waterfront shrimp docks and packing houses, including those of Ploeger Packing Company on the east side of Darien River bridge. At the foot of the north end of the bridge on the southwest corner of Walton and Broad streets is the Darien News building, formerly the old Georgia Coast & Piedmont Railroad depot. Directly across Broad Street is Jack Bluestein's supermarket and beyond that are other stores and businesses. The McIntosh County courthouse at the junction of US 17 and state 99 is correctly configured, as is the

124

Darien public school complex at upper right. I have many good memories of the days I spent in classrooms in these school buildings in the 1950s and early 60s. They have long since been replaced by more modern structures and the site is now the Middle School, with the high school having been moved several miles north on highway 17.

A Brief History of McIntosh County

The memoir in chapter 1, and the account of my rambles about McIntosh County, will almost certainly benefit from my providing some brief historical context, although ample history was noted in the previous chapter. What follows is a sketch of the county's human history as gleaned from my research and writings since 1985. Those seeking a more in-depth review and analysis are referred to the bibliography herein. The most complete compilation of the ecology, history, and culture of McIntosh County in a single volume, as well as covering other aspects of Georgia coastal history, is that found in my penultimate book, *Low Country Historian: A Collective Omnibus*, a new study published in 2023. It contains the latest revelations and findings from primary and secondary source materials relating to the subject, and I feel the volume is my definitive (i.e. most complete) history of the McIntosh area, to the extent that such a thing is possible considering all that has been written about the county by myself and other authors.

The earliest inhabitants were the Guale, part of the Lower Creeks. They were agriculturally advanced, with a presence on the mainland and offshore islands, such as Ossabaw, St. Catherines and Sapelo. Indian burial mounds and shell rings have been investigated by archaeologists on Sapelo. The first sustained European presence in what became McIntosh County was that of the Spanish missions beginning ca. 1570 and continuing for over a century. The missions on Sapelo Island and Talaje east of present-day Darien had interaction with the Guale until being forced south into Spanish Florida by 1684 due to English pressure from South Carolina. The English presence is therefore more recent, about three hundred years.[30]

---

[30] The literature of the Spanish presence from ca. 1570 to 1684 on the Guale coast of what became Georgia is extensive, much of it based on

In 1721, the later site of Darien was the setting for the first English settlement of the land that became Georgia when Fort King George was established near the mouth of the Altamaha River for the protection of South Carolina from potential Spanish incursions. Fifteen years later, in January 1736, a group of 180 Highlanders from Inverness, Scotland arrived at Lower Bluff, three years after the founding of the Georgia colony at Savannah by James Oglethorpe on behalf of the Georgia Trustees. Events were thus set in motion for the development of a permanent cultural legacy, among both blacks and whites, which has expanded to the present day.[31]

While their expertise was in military efficiency, hence their recruitment by Oglethorpe, the Scots were a resourceful, industrious people. Their new settlement, named Darien in honor of their fallen brethren in the Panamanian campaign a generation earlier, was both a military outpost, and a provider of beef and lumber for the colony's larger towns at Savannah and Frederica. It was the Highlanders, and their patriarchal leader, John McIntosh Mohr, who made important contributions to the survival and subsequent growth of the colony, not least of which was the leading role the Scots played in the defeat of the Spanish invasion of Georgia in 1742 at St. Simons Island.

With peace in 1748 came an end to the military necessity of Darien, and the settlers turned to agriculture and timber cutting as their economic livelihoods. The Scots settled on their grants of land throughout the newly designated St. Andrew Parish. It is important to note that in 1739, the original Darien Highlanders had composed a public petition against slavery being allowed in the Georgia colony. Nonetheless, slavery was legalized in the colony for the first time in 1750 and numbers of South Carolina rice and indigo planters moved

archaeological field research in the last fifty years. For a local overview see Buddy Sullivan, *Native American and Spanish Influences on McIntosh County, Georgia: An Archaeological Perspective* (privately published, 2019), which includes numerous bibliographical references to current and previous scholarly and field research. The outstanding scholarly studies are those by St. Catherines Island archaeologist David Hurst Thomas.

[31] Many books have been written about aspects of the history of McIntosh County. The most extensive reviews include five books by the present author: *Early Days on the Georgia Tidewater*, all editions, 1990-2019; *Darien, Georgia: A History of the Town & Its Environs* (privately published, 2020); *Sapelo: People and Place on a Georgia Sea Island* (Athens, 2017), and *Environmental Influences on Life & Labor in McIntosh County, Georgia: Case Studies in Ecology as History* (privately published, 2018, revised and updated, 2020), and the comprehensive *Low Country Historian*, noted above.

slaves and infrastructure to coastal Georgia, including the fertile rice lands of the Altamaha delta contiguous to Darien.

North and east of Darien, small farms were developed in proximity to the tidal rivers for convenience of transportation and communication. Much of the farming activity before and after the Revolutionary War occurred along the South Newport, Julianton and Sapelo rivers at places such as Harris Neck, White Chimney, Mallow (later Pine Harbor), Fair Hope and Belleville. Land grants of up to 500 and 1,000 acres were awarded in the northern sections of St. Andrew Parish to Sir Patrick Houstoun, Patrick Sutherland, William McIntosh, John McIntosh Mohr, William Thomas Harris, Daniel Demetre, Edward Baker, and others whose descendants would be prominent in northern McIntosh County for the next several generations.

Fort Barrington was built by the colonial authorities upriver on the Altamaha west of Darien to protect the landward side of the Parish; a dirt road was built connecting Darien with Savannah; and, in 1767, a survey by Lachlan McIntosh, son of John McIntosh Mohr, laid out the squares and street grid that would eventually become modern Darien. Lachlan McIntosh was the most famous of the clan for which the county was named, and that which settled Darien and St. Andrew Parish. The son of John McIntosh Mohr, he rose to become one of the leading figures in Georgia in the years before and during the Revolution. Despite a controversial duel with Declaration of Independence signer Button Gwinnett in 1777, McIntosh's star continued to rise; he became a general in the Continental Army, serving under Washington in the northern theater of the war, and later in the battles at Savannah and Charleston.

By an act of the Georgia legislature, McIntosh County was created in December 1793 with the seat of government established at Sapelo Bridge (present Eulonia) at the headwaters of the Sapelo River in the center of the new county. Darien at that time had not yet become an influential seaport and had fewer than one hundred residents and only a few businesses. During this period several New England citizens migrated to Darien and nearby St. Simons Island, including brothers Roswell King and Reuben King. They both became established leaders in the local community in agriculture, plantation management and business affairs.

In the antebellum period, the county was one of the most productive agricultural areas of the Georgia coast, largely as a consequence of its unique ecological and geographical situation on the tidewater, benefiting from water, soils and tides for the

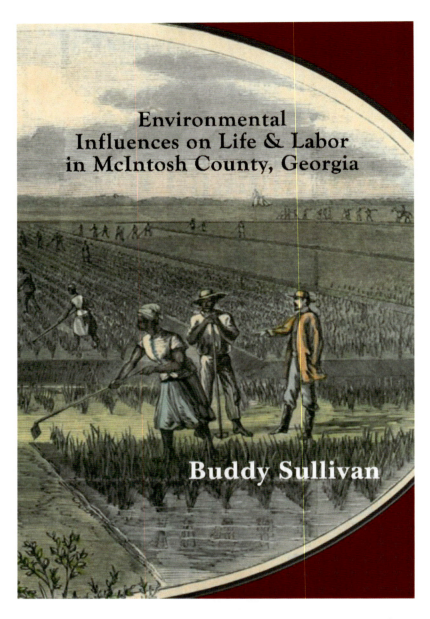

The cover of one of my books illustrating rice cultivation. From Harper's Weekly *in the 1860s. The sketch is of an unidentified Georgia plantation.*

commercial cultivation of money staples such as rice, cotton and sugar cane. These activities were based on the utilization of the task system of slave labor and resulted, for the most part, in efficiently managed, highly productive plantations which generated considerable wealth for the coastal planter class. The Altamaha River district, including the McIntosh and Glynn County sides of the river, and the lower Ogeechee River at present day Richmond Hill became centers of the Georgia rice economy from the 1830s to the 1870s.[32]

Combining the unique hydrological circumstances provided by ocean tides from the nearby Atlantic, and the fresh water flow from the upper Altamaha River, McIntosh County's rice plantations were among the most productive on the coast. The best-known of these was Butler's Island where Major Pierce Butler of Philadelphia, via South Carolina, began cultivation in 1790, eventually utilizing a slave force of 650 bondsmen that ultimately harvested as much as a million pounds of rice per year. Butler also produced cotton at Hampton plantation on St. Simons Island. He was the largest slaveholder in Georgia with a peak force of nearly one thousand slaves by 1830. The brick chimney for the old steam rice mill at Butler's Island still stands near Darien as a lasting legacy of the era of antebellum rice production on the Georgia coast. Butler's Island was later managed by the Major's grandson, Pierce Mease Butler whose wife, the celebrated English actress, Frances Anne Kemble, penned her acclaimed *Journal of a Residence on a Georgian Plantation in 1838-1839*, which, when published in 1863, was the severest indictment of American slavery since the works of Harriet Beecher Stowe. She visited Butler's Island and St. Simons Island accompanying her husband for several months in 1838-39 and conducted interviews with many of the enslaved people on the two estates during the course of her observations and written accounts.

Other leading rice producers were Thomas Bryan Forman (Broughton Island), Jacob Barrett (Champneys Island), Robert B. Rhett (Rhett's Island), and Charles Spalding and P.M. Nightingale (Cambers Island). On Cathead Creek, an Altamaha tributary west of Darien with headwaters in the expansive Buffalo Swamp, were

---

[32] The coastal rice industry of the early-to-mid nineteenth century is covered extensively in several of the books by Buddy Sullivan, chiefly *Low Country Historian: A Collective Omnibus* (privately published, 2023); *Environmental Influences on Life & Labor in McIntosh County, Georgia* (privately published, 2020); *Life & Labor on Butler's Island: Rice Cultivation in the Altamaha Delta* (privately published, 2019); and *From Beautiful Zion to Red Bird Creek: A History of Bryan County, Georgia* (Pembroke, GA, 2000). The author drew extensively on contemporary journals, manuscript records and account books, and census data to document his studies of the rice plantations.

smaller rice plantations owned and managed by such families as Dunwody, Smith, Morris, Mallard and Gignilliat. On the Glynn side were the Hofwyl plantation of the Troup and Dent families, and Hopeton, managed by James Hamilton Couper as the most efficient and productive plantation in the South according, in 1832, to the *Southern Agriculturalist*, the premier farm journal of the day.

The leading citizen of McIntosh County in the antebellum period was Thomas Spalding of Sapelo Island and Ashantilly. A "scientific farmer" who introduced experimentation, crop diversification and innovation to agriculture, Spalding (1774-1851) developed a plantation empire on Sapelo and was regarded as one of the leading agrarians in America. At Sapelo, Spalding was a highly successful cotton producer, and introduced the commercial manufacture of sugar to Georgia, building the state's first sugar mill in 1809. He was an enthusiastic advocate of the use of tabby as a building material, developing his own "formula" for making oyster shell tabby, and unselfishly sharing his concepts with his fellow planters through his numerous contributions to agricultural journals. Spalding was the second largest slaveholder in the McIntosh County to the Butler estate, was known as a liberal and humane slave owner, and most unusually, had a black overseer, Muhammad Bilali, as his plantation manager at Sapelo. Spalding was an enthusiastic promotor of railroad and canal development in Georgia and was an untiring advocate of the concept of "localism" in promoting Darien and the Georgia coast as a whole as a whole as Southern economic centers. He was also a stateman, serving briefly in the U.S. House of Representatives and the Georgia general assembly, and was a committed Unionist in opposing Southern secession in the years before his death.[33]

In the early 1800s, northern shipbuilders cut live oak timber on Blackbeard Island for the purpose of building warships for early U.S. Navy. Unpopulated Blackbeard became a Navy Department timber reserve following its acquisition from the short-lived French company that attempted to develop adjoining Sapelo Island from 1790-1795. Blackbeard was later utilized by the U.S. Marine Hospital Service as a yellow fever quarantine inspection station. The station was on Sapelo Sound when that harbor was a major outlet for Darien-processed

---

[33] Spalding is covered in depth in the studies cited in the previous footnote, as well as Buddy Sullivan, *Thomas Spalding, Antebellum Planter of Sapelo* (privately published, 2019), and Sullivan, *Sapelo: People and Place on a Georgia Sea Island* (Athens: University of Georgia Press, 2017).

pine timber for the international shipping arriving to take on cargoes. The quarantine station operated from 1880 to 1910 when it was deactivated, and Blackbeard was soon after designated as a federal wildlife refuge which it remains to the present day.[34]

On the McIntosh mainland, sea island cotton cultivation flourished despite damaging hurricanes in 1804 and 1824. Families such as Hopkins (Belleville), Atwood (Cedar Point), Nephew (Manchester-Valona, and Cathead Creek), Smith (Thicket and Sidon), Kell (Laurel Grove), and Wylly (Thicket and the Forest) were prominent cotton producers. Beginning in 1816, the sugar mill and rum distillery of William Carnochan at the Thicket northeast of Darien (with input from Thomas Spalding's expertise in tabby) was an important business until the operation was destroyed in the 1824 hurricane. The tabby ruins of the mill works and slave dwellings are still in evidence at the Thicket, now a residential community. There was a good deal of inter-marriage among many of the leading families of the agricultural class of McIntosh, for example Brailsford-Troup-Dent (Hofwyl), Brailsford-Spalding Sutherland's Bluff and Sapelo), Spalding-Wylly, Hopkins-King, Gignilliat-Mallard, Harris-Thorpe, and Thomas-Houstoun, among others.[35]

At Harris Neck, in the northeast section of the county, large cotton plantations were owned by the families of Francis Levett at Julianton, David Delegal and his descendants at Delta, Jonathan Thomas at Peru, William John King at Harris Neck. and the descendants of William Thomas Harris. Along the South Newport River were the smaller, but productive cotton tracts of James E. Houstoun at Marengo, James Gignilliat and Edward P. Postell at Belvedere, Charles C. Thorpe at Lebanon, and the McDonald and McIntosh families at South Newport. Creighton Island was the scene of extensive cotton production in the antebellum period, as were Manchester, Cedar Point and the Meadows on the mainland opposite the island. On the Sapelo River were the plantations of Daniel H. Brailsford at Sutherland's Bluff, Reuben King at Mallow, Alexander Wylly at the Forest, and William J. McIntosh and Daniel McDonald at Fair Hope, in addition to smaller farm tracts at

---

[34] Utilizing federal archival sources Blackbeard is covered in detail by the author in all of the previously-cited studies.

[35] For a review of the most prominent colonial and antebellum families of the county, see the previous studies cited in earlier notes, and Buddy Sullivan, *Early Families of McIntosh County, Georgia, 1736-1861* (privately published, 2020).

White Chimney River near Shellman Bluff in north McIntosh County.

Shellman Bluff (William Cooke), and nearby White Chimney (Cannon, Durant and Forbes families). Many of the north McIntosh County families had multiple generations managing the plantation and farm tracts in the section. William Cooke and his brother-in-law Charles H. Spalding had sizeable cotton operations on the north end of Creighton Island, which had convenient water access to Sapelo Sound and the Sutherland's Bluff-Shellman plantation tracts.[36]

On the south end of the county, the McIntosh County seat of government was moved from Sapelo Bridge to Darien on the north branch of the Altamaha River in 1818 in response to the town's rapid growth as a cotton and rice shipping center in the first two decades of the nineteenth century. Regular steamboat service between Milledgeville, the state capital on the Oconee River, and Darien, was established in 1819. Upcountry cotton barged down the Altamaha was shipped from Darien in such quantities that, by 1832, the port was exporting about half the state's cotton at a time when Georgia was the leading producer of that commodity in the world. Darien's commercial prosperity was such that the Bank of Darien, after its charter in 1818, became one of the leading financial institutions in the eastern United States.

Darien was bypassed by railroad development in the 1830s and 1840s and the town entered economic depression as most of the interior cotton began to be shipped by rail to Savannah and Charleston. The Bank of Darien lost its state charter and was closed in 1842 largely due to the loss of the interior cotton trade. After 1840, the main agricultural staple shipped to the bigger markets was rice from the delta plantations. However, lumber and naval stores production became important economic mainstays by the 1850s and Darien's saw mills at Lower Bluff on the Darien River and the Upper Mill on Cathead Creek were active in producing lumber from pine timber rafted down the Altamaha from the interior.

McIntosh County suffered greatly in the Civil War. Many of the county's plantations were destroyed during Union naval raids on the Sapelo River. The coast was blockaded by federal warships in Sapelo, Doboy and Altamaha sounds. The war hit Darien the hardest. In one of the most controversial incidents of the war, the undefended and largely deserted town was looted, and then burned by attacking

---

[36] Buddy Sullivan, *Harris Neck & Its Environs: A History of North McIntosh County* (privately published, 2020), containing much the same text in the author's previously cited studies, with new material.

Pine timber rafts from the Altamaha upcountry being inspected at Darien.

Union forces in June 1863, with hardly any structures left standing in the wake of the devastation.

Immediately after the war, aided by an infusion of Northern capital, Darien quickly rebuilt its economic fortunes partly on a revived rice industry in the Altamaha delta, but more importantly on a rapidly growing timber prosperity. The demand for Georgia pine timber and lumber from overseas and the northeast U.S. made Darien prosperous once again during the years of Reconstruction and afterwards. The saw mills were rebuilt, largely through an infusion of northern capital, timber began flowing down the Altamaha once again and ships arrived from Europe, South America and New England to load raw timber and processed lumber from the local mills. The leaders of this growth were the mills and shipping operations of Joseph Hilton and his family. Hilton developed large-scale lumber operations at Lower Bluff, the Upper Mill at Cathead, and at Doboy Island, the latter for the convenience of larger sailing vessels with too much draft to navigate the shallow rivers to the Darien mills. Starting in 1889, Sapelo Sound became the primary timber loading ground for foreign shipping for steamships and sailing ships from Great Britain and Scandinavia. The three largest Darien timber firms—Hilton & Dodge, Hunter-Benn and James K. Clarke—set up loading docks off the Sound on small hammocks along Front River (Creighton Island marshes) and Julianton River (near lower Harris Neck). The most active of these anchorages was Hazzard's hammock at the juncture of Front River and Sapelo Sound. Additionally, the Darien Short Line Railroad was developed by local investors in 1889-90 to ship timber from Tattnall and Liberty counties to Belleville landing on the Sapelo River, earmarked for Sapelo Sound shipping. Darien had its first rail connection when the Short Line was extended twelve miles from Crescent to Darien in 1895. The Sapelo Sound shipping trade ended in 1914 with the decline of timber availability.

Darien was the second-leading timber port in the United States (behind only Pensacola), and the industry provided employment opportunities as stevedores, raftsmen, mill operators, and bar pilots. Blacks and whites alike thus acquired jobs in the difficult economic times after the war. As a result of timber, McIntosh County realized recovery more rapidly than other areas of the South. It is also important to remember that this activity spanning fifty years solidified the county's maritime heritage in the truest sense.

The peak year of the timber economy was 1900 when a record 112.5 million board feet of timber was exported from Darien, Doboy and Front River. But the local timber prosperity ended as suddenly as it had begun, however. Due to the overcutting of the upriver forests, timber rafted to Darien was reduced to a trickle by 1915 and the local mills gradually ceased operations. From the peak in 1900, shipments of raw timber and processed lumber from the Darien mills declined to 16.5 million board feet in 1910. The Hilton-Dodge lumber empire went bankrupt in 1916, and its Lower Bluff saw mill ceased operations in 1923. Even the extension of the Georgia Coast & Piedmont Railroad from Darien to Brunswick in 1914 could not save the timber industry. The G.C. & P. went bankrupt in 1920, with the track being removed to build an automobile road from Brunswick to Darien. It opened to traffic in 1921, and eventually became U.S. Highway 17 through McIntosh County and coastal Georgia.[37]

It is important to note the development of African American communities in McIntosh County after the Civil War. The emancipated slaves returned to the plantations in large numbers and purchased land from their former owners to establish permanent

---

[37] For a comprehensive review of railroad development and the nineteenth century timber industry, the author's previously cited studies should be consulted.

Photograph, 1932, of the two Sapelo Island lighthouses. The steel light in the background was deactivated and dismantled in 1934.

settlements and develop their own independent farming activities. Several hundred freedmen settled on Sapelo Island as they acquired land from the Spalding descendants, and communities such as Raccoon Bluff, Hog Hammock, Shell Hammock, Lumber Landing and Belle Marsh had their own distinct identities and populations. By 1910, the U.S. census counted 510 African Americans living in a dozen scattered communities on Sapelo, many of the people being slave descendants from the Spalding era.

Other freedmen communities were established through the purchase of lands on the north end of Harris Neck from the heirs of the Thomas, Harris, King and Delegal families. Darien also had a large African American community, especially helped by the timber industry. Tunis G. Campbell, an African American official of the Freedmen's Bureau, developed a powerful political base in McIntosh County from 1868 to 1876; he and members of his family became the first black representatives to the state legislature from McIntosh.

The county's economic dynamics began to change in the first decades of the twentieth century. With the end of the timber industry, many blacks, and later whites as well, turned to the harvest of seafood. The oyster industry was especially viable in the county from 1890 to 1940 and the commercial processing of oysters was facilitated at canneries at Darien (Ploeger-Abbott Company), Valona (William H. Kittles), Cedar Point (Atwood family) and Harris Neck (Augustus Oemler).

A brick vault built in the 1920s for the Warsaw Lumber Company is all that remains of the saw mill settlement on the Seaboard railroad.

In the 1930s, the shrimping industry began to flourish. McIntosh County's shrimp boat fleet expanded to become the largest on the Georgia coast, particularly in the two decades following the Second World War. McIntosh County shrimping families were among the state's leaders in the industry, and included such early producers as Thorpe, Baker, Todd, Boone, Durant, Burrows, Watson, Atwood, Ward, Brannen, Ploeger and Gale. The county's shrimping communities such as Darien, Meridian, Valona, Cedar Point and Belleville, had large trawler fleets from the 1950s through the 1970s, the peak years of the local industry.

In the western section of McIntosh, there was a brief revival of the timber and naval stores industry thanks to the development of railroads in coastal Georgia. In the early 1900s new communities such as Townsend, Warsaw, Jones and Cox sprouted up along the Seaboard Air Line Railway. The Warsaw Lumber Company north of Townsend was one of the largest producers of pine lumber in coastal Georgia in the 1920s and 1930s before the mill closed and the community disappeared almost overnight as people moved away. The production of turpentine from pine rosin was an important economic mainstay for the county from the early 1900s to the 1950s.

From 1916 to 1925 the Georgia Land & Livestock Company acquired thousands of acres of pine flatwoods in the western and northern sections of McIntosh County for a proposed large-scale cattle-raising venture that was ultimately unsuccessful.

On Sapelo Island, first Howard E. Coffin (1873-1937), then Richard J. Reynolds, Jr. (1906-1964) were owners of the majority of the island's land from 1912 until state acquisition of the island in two purchases from the Reynolds estate in 1969 and 1976. Coffin, a Detroit automotive executive and engineer, energized Sapelo with his agricultural, seafood, road building, and construction projects, employing many of Sapelo's African American residents. Coffin understood the importance of coastal conservation and developed oversight of thousands of acres of marshlands in McIntosh County to promote a more sustainable oyster industry. With his younger cousin Alfred W. Jones, Coffin established the Sea Island Company in 1926 on Sea Island adjacent to St. Simons Island, and built the world-class Cloister resort hotel, aiming to attract affluent Northerners to coastal Georgia rather than Florida for their vacations. Financial realities brought on by the Depression forced Coffin to sell Sapelo to Reynolds in 1934. He turned over the Sea Island venture to Jones.[38] During Reynolds' ownership, modern buildings were constructed, telephone service was implemented, and partial ferry service was begun.

In 1953, Reynolds provided facilities to the University of Georgia to open a marine research station. It evolved into the UGA Marine Institute, becoming one of the leading facilities in the world for salt marsh and estuarine scientific research. From 1954 to the early 2000s such ecological scientific luminaries as Eugene P. Odum (universally acknowledged as the "father of estuarine ecology"), John Teal, and R.A. Ragotzskie pursued investigations into the dynamics of the salt marshes surrounding Sapelo. The results and importance of their findings proved that the detritus from decaying marshes provided life-giving sustenance to an array of shellfish such as shrimp, oysters and crabs, thus providing the impetus for the coastal commercial fishery. The science from UGAMI researchers and others led to important state legislation in 1970 (Coastal Marshlands Protection Act) that provided buffers against proposed mining, development and other harmful practices relating to the tidal

---

[38] The Coffin era on Sapelo, 1912-1934, and the early development of Sea Island by Coffin and A.W. Jones are covered in detail in the author's previously cited studies.

The research laboratory at Sapelo Island's Marine Institute was once the R.J. Reynolds dairy barn.

marshes of Georgia. Despite a short coastline, Georgia has more salt marsh acreage than any other east coast state.[39]

Reynolds died in 1964 but not before he had consolidated the island's Geechee communities through a series of land exchanges to create one island community at Hog Hammock—an action that remains controversial to the present day for the descendants of earlier generations of families who had lived at Raccoon Bluff, Shell Hammock and other communities. In two transactions in 1969 and 1976, the state of Georgia acquired ownership of most of the land on Sapelo which it retains to the present day.

The economic focus of McIntosh County began gradually evolving during the 1980s and 1990s. The decline of the seafood industry, particularly shrimping, hurt the county economically. Although shrimping remains an important commercial activity for McIntosh, many people have become employed by the growing service industry in the county, from tourism, short-term visitation and seasonal residency.

---

[39] See the last chapter of this book for a discussion of low country ecosystems, especially the salt marshes of McIntosh County.

From the 1980s to the present, an influx of new residents has come into McIntosh County, many of them retirees or near-retirees, to establish permanent homes. This trend has been especially prevalent in the northern sections of the county with the growth of such one-time sleepy communities as Shellman Bluff, Contentment, Pine Harbor and Fairhope, and new affluent sections in those areas such as Sutherland's Bluff, Belvedere, Springfield, Cooper's Point and Delta. The population of the county in 2020 was about 14,000 residents, not including a large number of seasonal residents.

The beach at Blackbeard Island, looking south toward Sapelo Island.

Place Names for a Lifetime[40]

*A**ltamaha River*–A name referenced as early as 1540 in the chronicles of the Spanish expedition of Hernando DeSoto through Georgia. Altamaha is an Indian name related to the Creek village of *Tama* inland from the coast at the fork of the Oconee and Ocmulgee rivers where they meet to form the Altamaha. The Indian terminology of *Al-Tama* refers to "on the way to Tama." Until the early 19th century, the river was often spelled on maps with an extra "a" as in *Alatamaha.*

Ashantilly–Named by James Spalding, father of Thomas Spalding of Sapelo, for the ancestral home of the Spalding family in Perthshire, Scotland, that being the Barony of Ashantilly.

Baisden's Bluff–Possibly named for Josiah Baisden, a McIntosh County citizen in the 1790s who may have resided at the bluff on the Crescent (South Sapelo) River.

Barbour Island–Named for John Barbour ("Barber" in some colonial and antebellum documents), original grantee of the island in 1767.

Beacon Creek (Wolf Island)–Between the beach and marsh of upper Wolf Island. The head of this tidal creek was near the range beacon that operated from 1822 to 1898.

Behavior (Sapelo Island)–Traditional. Supposedly named by Thomas Spalding upon awarding food and livestock to slaves who had run away provided they agreed to return to work. Behavior was a slave settlement, then later an African American cemetery, which it remains to this day.

Belleville–Named by Captain John McIntosh, the original grantee of the tract ca. 1750, later owned by his daughter Catherine and son-in-law, George Troup. Their sons were two of McIntosh County's most historic figures—James McGillivray Troup, and George Michael Troup. See Index for references to both.

Belvedere Island–Likely named by John McDonald, original grantee of the island in 1758, but possibly by James Gignilliat who acquired the tract ca. 1793.

---

[40] The following pages relate the historical origins of the many places in McIntosh County that have been associated with my research.

Black Island–Named by John McIntosh Mohr, leader of the Highland Scots who founded Darien, and the first grantee of the tract. It was named for Black Isle near Inverness in Scotland's Cromarty Firth, from whence the Highlanders came to Georgia. The origin of the local use of the place name "Mayhall" was established by the research of county historian Bessie M. Lewis. She made a logical connection between Mayhall Island and its larger neighbor to the west across Mayhall Creek and marsh, Black Island. Miss Lewis wrote in the *Darien News* in 1975 that "Often we have wondered about Black Island, called by that name when it was granted to John Mohr McIntosh in the 1750s. Most of the early Highland settlers of Darien came from the vicinity of Inverness, near where the lovely Black Isle lies green across the Cromarty Firth. What could be more natural than that they should give that name to the island just over the creek from Barnwell's Bluff from whence they first saw the site of their new home in Georgia? As for the small island beside Black Island, it had no name when it was granted to John Mohr McIntosh. Now it is called Mayhall, or Myhall. But on some of the older maps it appears as Moy Hall. When one remembers that the ancestral home of the Mackintosh of Mackintosh was Moy Hall, a castle on an island, it does not seem strange that John Mohr McIntosh should have this small island in the Altamaha named Moy Hall. Often I have wondered if an archaeological investigation might disclose evidence that his home was actually on Moy instead of Black Island."

Blackbeard Island–Named for the early 18th century pirate Edward Teach—more familiarly known as Blackbeard—who allegedly hid his loot on the island, though none has ever been found. Earliest documented use of this place name was on a 1760 survey of neighboring Sapelo Island.

Blue and Hall Landing–Named for Alexander Blue and John H. Hall who in the 1850s operated a saw mill on the site fronting the North River between the Thicket and the Ridge.

Bourbon Field (Sapelo Island)–Owned and possibly named by French royalist Picot de Boisfeillet ca. 1790.

Brickstone–A brick-making plant on the Seaboard railroad between Jones and Townsend. Pronounced *Brix-tun*, the factory ceased operations in 1918 and the settlement disappeared.

Broughton Island–A rice island in the lower Altamaha delta granted to Jonathan Bryan in 1758. Likely named for Thomas Broughton, lieutenant governor of South Carolina who was associated with Oglethorpe. Savannah's well-known Broughton Street was also named for him.

Bruro Neck and River–Named for Brora, part of the Sutherland family holdings in Scotland. Lieutenant Patrick Sutherland of Oglethorpe's regiment was granted land in its lower portion, the tract that came to be known as Sutherland's Bluff, following the War of Jenkins Ear with Spain.

Butler's Island–Named upon acquisition of the tidal island in 1784 by Major Pierce Butler.

Camber's Island–Named in association with Thomas Camber who was granted the tract in 1762.

Cannon Bluff–Named for the Cannon family who settled and farmed the tract on the west side of the White Chimney River in the antebellum period and afterwards.

Carneghan–Named for William Carnochan, sugar planter at the nearby Thicket, early 1800s.

Cat Head, Cathead Creek–Named by Highland Scots for Clan Chattan of St. Cattan's, "Little Cat."

Cedar Point–A grant to John Lachlan McIntosh, who named the tract for the abundance of cedar trees along the nearby creek. It was inherited by his daughter, Ann Margaret McIntosh, who married Henry S. Atwood in 1824. The Oak Hill tract comprised lands from Crescent to Meridian, including Cedar Point.

Champneys Island–Named for John Champneys of South Carolina who acquired the tract following the American Revolution.

Chocolate (Sapelo Island)–Derived from "Chucalate," a Guale village on Sapelo's North End.

Columbus Square (Darien)–Named for Christopher Columbus, Italian explorer.

Contentment Bluff–Probably named by James Gignilliat upon his acquisition of the tract on Bruro Neck north of Shellman Bluff after the Revolution.

Cow Horn Road–Early name for present-day state highway 99. A look at any map and the route of the road from Darien to Eulonia will easily divulge how the road got its name.

Cox–Named for a member of the Cox family in the early 1900s, likely Samuel Cox (1887-1943), who was possibly an early settler there. He is buried in the Gardner-Poppell Cemetery near Cox. With its turpentine distillery and saw mill, Cox became a stop on the Seaboard railroad.

Creighton Island–Named for British Loyalist Alexander Creighton of Savannah who acquired the island from the Habersham family during the Revolution.

Crescent–Named for the "crescent bend" of the nearby Crescent River, delineated on some maps as South Sapelo River. Crescent River is the preferred usage locally, and is the name used on NOAA charts.

Darien–Named by the Highlanders in honor of their fellow Scots who perished at the failed colony of Darien on the Isthmus of Panama.

Delta–Named by David Delegal, original grantee of the Harris Neck tract in 1771. *Delta* may have been an intentional derivative of *Delegal.*

Doboy Island and Doboy Sound–Named for Jehan Duboys (or Dubois), a French navigator who investigated the area in 1564. Anglicized to *Doboy* shortly after establishment of the Georgia colony.

Eulonia–Formerly Sapelo Bridge, Eulonia was so named in 1895 upon application for a post office by O.S. Davis who had migrated to McIntosh County from Eulonia, S.C.

Fairhope–Originally a grant to William McIntosh who named his plantation on the Sapelo River Fair Hope (two words) ca. 1750.

General's Island–Named for General Lachlan McIntosh who was granted the rice tract before the Revolution.

Gould's Landing (Harris Neck)–The Gould plantation, Bahama, was here on the Barbour Island River.

Hanging Bull (Sapelo Island)–Traditional. Origin unknown. The place name appears in French ownership documents as early as 1794.

Hazzard's hammock, Sapelo Sound–Named for William Hazzard who operated a store on the small hammock where ships deposited rock ballast and loaded timber conveyed from Darien, 1889 to 1914.

Hird Island–Granted to Thomas Hird of Frederica in 1743.

Hog Hammock (Sapelo Island)–Traditional. Supposedly named for Sampson Hogg, a Spalding plantation slave who managed livestock on the tract that evolved as an island settlement after 1865.

Hudson–Captain John Hudson's plantation was on the tract in the early 1800s.

Jones–Named for Samuel Jones whose farm was there before the Revolution. Jonesville, later Jones, became a summer retreat for planter families of lower Liberty County.

Julianton (Harris Neck) and River–On the lower end of Harris Neck, named for Juliana, mother of Francis Levett; he owned a cotton plantation on the tract until his death in 1802. Often mis-spelled as "Julienton" (with an "e") or "Julington" on maps and documents even to the present day.

Kittles Island–William H. Kittles of Valona and his heirs owned this hammock on Atwood Creek for most of the 20th century. Adjacent to Maxine Island, renamed Seabreeze upon development in the 1980s.

Mayhall Island–Granted to John McIntosh Mohr, leader of the Darien Scots who named the tract for Moy Hall, a Scottish castle and ancestral home of the McIntoshes. Long-time locals often pronounce the island's name as *My-Hall* and appears on some early maps as such. See also Black Island above.

Meridian–Ostensibly named by Reuben King Hopkins who applied for a post office, and was appointed postmaster thereof, in 1896.

Oldnor Island–Named for Richard Oldnor, granted the small tract during the colonial period.

Old Teakettle Creek–Origin unknown. The name appears as early as 1760 on the Sapelo Island survey.

Patterson Island–Named for Robert Patterson, early 19th century owner of the tract on Woodlands (later Atwood) Creek. Patterson's widow, Frances Patterson, married John Lafong, a Frenchman who cultivated crops on Patterson Island until his death in 1819.

Pico Cut–Tradition has the cut in the Darien River south of Lower Bluff named for Pico de Boisfeillet, a French businessman and Sapelo Island investor. He briefly lived in Darien until his death in 1800.

Pine Harbor–Named by surveyor Ravenel Gignilliat in 1916. Pine Harbor is on the site of the Mallow plantation on the Sapelo River, and the short-lived development called the Fairhope Land Company in 1911.

Potosi Island–West of Darien, apparently named by rice and sugar cane planter Jacob Wood ca. 1800 for the silver mining city of Potosi in Bolivia.

Priester–On the Julianton River, named ca. 1886 for a tract awarded to Emma Stebbins Priester and her husband John N. Priester, by her father Charles Stebbins, Jr. Originally part of Marengo plantation.

Raccoon Bluff (Sapelo Island)–Origin unknown. It appears in French documents as early as 1792.

Rhett's Island–Originally part of General's Island, it was acquired by Robert Barnwell Rhett in 1856 for rice cultivation. Rhett's and General's islands are separated by General's Cut.

Rifle Cut–A narrow man-made waterway "as straight as a rifle shot" connecting the main branch of the Altamaha River with the Darien River west of Darien. Dug in the 1820s to expedite the movement of timber to the Darien saw mills.

Rockdedundy Island and River–Literally *Rock of Dundee* in Scotland–another of the many local place names that are Scottish in origin.

Rock Island–On Doboy Sound near Doboy Island. Its name comes for the line of hammocks created where ballast stone was deposited by European timber ships in the 19th century.

Sapelo–Native American in origin as *Capala* according to 16th century Spanish records. Named *Sapala* by the Spanish, *Sapola* by the French, before being anglicized about 1735. Early English spellings had the island spelled with an ending "e," as *Sapeloe,* a spelling used again during the H.E. Coffin ownership.

Shell Bluff–Original name for Valona. Part of the fishing community is situated on Shellbluff Creek.

Shellman Bluff–Originally *Shellman,* an antebellum cotton plantation on the site overlooking Bruro River, one of the 19th century Spalding family holdings.

Springfield–A common plantation name in the Georgia and South Carolina low country.

Sutherland's Bluff–Named for the colonial grantee of the tract, Patrick Sutherland, military officer in Oglethorpe's service in the war with Spain.

Tolomato–Named for the 17th century Spanish mission *Tolomato,* originally, but incorrectly thought to be located on the tract of the present residential community northeast of Darien. The Tolomato mission was actually at Harris Neck.

Townsend–Named for Joseph E. Townsend who acquired the railroad rights-of-way through western McIntosh County from the mid-to-late 1880s.

Union Island–Known as Pumpkin Hammock before and after the Civil War and continued to appear as such on maps into the early 1900s.

Valona–Named for post office purposes in 1898 by George E. Atwood for the seaport of Valona, Albania from which vessels came to local waters for timber. Formerly known as Shell Bluff, part of the Manchester tract. Valona, and neighboring Cedar Point, have always been associated with the Atwood family.

Vernon Square–Named for Admiral Edward Vernon (1684-1757), who served in the War of Jenkins Ear.

146

Wahoo Island–Granted to John Barbour in 1767, possibly named by him. Wahoo is the name for both a large gamefish in sub-tropical waters, and an eastern U.S. shrub or small tree.

Warsaw–Named in 1915, replacing the earlier name of Darien Junction where two railroads intersected—the Seaboard Air Line and the Georgia Coast & Piedmont. Scene of large-scale saw mill operations in the 1920s and 1930s. The settlement disappeared when timber activity ended by 1940.

White Chimney–Origin uncertain for the tract and the tidal river. Identified as the "White Chimneys" in local deeds as early as the 1830s.

Wright's Island–Colonial grant to Sir James Wright, third royal governor of Georgia.

Young's Island–Named for the Young family that had been settled on the central McIntosh County tract between U.S. 17 and Warsaw since the mid-1800s.

"A Forever Sense of Place"
My *Low Country Environment*

The closing chapter of this memoir of the low country is intended to provide a sense of the uniqueness of where we are. Throughout the years of my work, and in virtually every book, the thematic intent has been to emphasize the significance of *place* in our coastal culture—now and in all the past generations of those who have inhabited the Georgia coast. *Place* in this context relates to the environment of one's surroundings and how one associates with those surroundings. This concept obviously applies to everyone who lives anywhere on the planet, but of course low country Georgia is the focus here and it is where I want to relate my own understanding of where we are and how we got here through science and discovery.

Ecology, for the purposes of the following discussion, entails the salt marshes and their tidal cycles, and the biological and chemical processes within those elements, along with other local ecological considerations: soil types, river hydrology, etc. To properly understand the history and geography of the low country, and particularly that of McIntosh County, it is instructive to have a grasp of its ecological characteristics.

The present stands of the Georgia coastal marshes that form wide swaths between the barrier islands and the mainland are well developed, and have been relatively stable for the last five thousand years as *Holocene* formations. Earlier late-*Pleistocene* marshes, however, underwent frequent change, even disappearing altogether at times in response to alterations in sea level that created unstable conditions. With adequate sea level heights in the Holocene, water-borne sediments were deposited on underlying Pleistocene sediments to build new marshes and beaches over the earlier ones. Clays and fine sands make up the marsh deposits that form in the sheltered areas away from the direct impacts of the sea, accounting for the stable marsh belts along Sapelo Island's west side and south end, between Sapelo and Blackbeard islands, and between those two islands and the mainland several miles to the west.[41] Another destabilizing cycle may currently be in progress in light of evidence of pronounced sea level rise along the south Atlantic shoreline.

The Georgia coast, about one hundred miles in length, features a distinct island chain separated from the mainland by a four-to-six-mile wide belt of marshes. From east to west, the islands feature sand beaches, dune lines, and a slightly-elevated interior forest often dissected by tidal sloughs and freshwater ponds. Penetrated by creeks and rivers, the marshes extend westward to the coastal mainland. On its eastern edge the mainland is only slightly elevated, but is buffered from the direct effects of tropical storms by the marshes and islands. Freshwater rivers—the Savannah, Ogeechee, Altamaha, Satilla, and St. Marys—empty into the Atlantic Ocean through sounds that separate the islands. A sequence of salt, brackish, and freshwater marshes follow the river channels upstream into areas of decreasing salinity.

An ocean current, the longshore littoral current, evolves counterclockwise off the Gulf Stream, flowing from north to south along the shorelines of Blackbeard, Sapelo and Wolf islands in McIntosh County, and producing a regular movement of sand to the southward. The littoral current mixes with a strong outflow current from Doboy Sound south of Sapelo that moves from northwest to southeast on ebbing tides. The sandbars, beaches and dunes of lower Blackbeard and Sapelo's Cabretta Island and Nanny Goat Beach are regularly altered by a combination of currents, tide flow and wind

---

[41] J.R. Hails and J.H. Hoyt, "An Appraisal of the Evolution of the Lower Atlantic Coastal Plain of Georgia," *Proceedings* of the Institute of British Geographers 46 (1969): 53-68.

conditions. Simultaneously, the accretion of sands washed southward from Blackbeard accumulate on the beaches on the southern end of Sapelo with additional buildup of marsh west of the dunes and on the lighthouse tract. This natural "sand-sharing" process makes Sapelo Island one of the few remaining places on the east coast where the phenomenon is evolving with minimal interference from human activity.

The shoreline changes can be readily observed from a study of topographic maps and navigation charts of the area over the last two hundred years in which there is a progressive erosion of the north end of Blackbeard Island with a concomitant accretion of beach on Sapelo's South End. There are sharply eroded, truncated dune ridges on the north end of Blackbeard with much of their sediment eventually being deposited on the lower part of Sapelo where the beaches are pro-grading and the dunes are increasing in size. Both islands have shifted southward about 0.75 mile during the present Holocene high stand of the sea. At the same time, the accumulation of sand on Sapelo's South End has created natural obstacles to the Doboy Sound entrance with continually-shifting shoals and sandbars, not all of which are exposed at low tide—hence the numerous shipwrecks and ship groundings that have been recorded over the last two centuries by traffic approaching the inlet. Some of the sand from Nanny Goat Beach is also washed southward by the prevailing winds and currents. The cycle of erosion and accretion is constant, with sand eroded from one area of beach to be deposited in the offshore sandbars, then being washed back onto the beach with the resultant buildup of dunes.

The beach itself is composed of fine quartz sands mixed with small amounts of crushed shell. On Nanny Goat, the beach slopes gradually from the dune base to the water's edge, varying in width with its narrowest portion on the north across the inlet from Cabretta Island. Typical of the gently shelving southeastern shoreline, the water is very shallow for a considerable distance offshore from Sapelo, averaging only about eight feet a mile from the beach at mean low water.

The changing dynamics of the Georgia islands that are in federal or state administration, or those that remain in private ownership such as St. Catherines Island, do not affect people as there is no development on these islands near beach areas; it can, however, be detrimental to nesting areas for turtles and shorebirds such as the American Oystercatcher, Wilson's Plover, Least Tern, Gull-billed

Tern, and Black Skimmer. These species rely on the stability of the beaches near the high tide line to lay their eggs.

During the summer months, marine turtles regularly nest and lay their eggs on the barrier island beaches and dunes, particularly those with minimal human use or impacts, the most prevalent species being the Atlantic loggerhead (*Caretta caretta caretta*). From May to early September the female loggerheads move to the beach at night, often during the flood stage of a spring tide, to lay from 120 to 130 eggs on dry ground close to the dune line. Most of the eggs fall victim to natural predators, but some hatchlings survive and return to the sea. Other large marine turtles may have nested on Sapelo in the past, including the Atlantic hawksbill, Atlantic green, and Atlantic leatherback.

Beach sand dunes are quite fragile; new dunes nearest the beach are the most unstable, and are under constant alteration by "blowout" from strong winds, and "washover" from a combination of storm waves and northeasterly winds. Dune buildup near the beaches typically occurs in periods of calm weather with onshore winds. As seen from the air, the lower end of Nanny Goat Beach on Sapelo reveals dune lines in large arcs curving around the southern tip of the beach with sand accruing in the embayment washed by Doboy Sound's currents, lying just southeast of the lighthouse.

When constructed in the early nineteenth century, the lighthouse was on an island sand spit separated by a creek from the main island. Like Nanny Goat Beach, the lighthouse spit is Holocene but is positioned well behind the beaches and dunes; it is also subject to accretion, but in a different way. Nineteenth and early twentieth century maps and photographs reveal a gradual buildup of marshes projecting south of the lighthouse: a 1932 photograph of the tower places it very near the waters of Doboy Sound whereas marshes have since filled in a considerable area south of the tower, a clear illustration of the buildup of the South End through the sand-sharing system.

Sapelo Island has two distinct lines of sand dunes, with the inter-dune meadow in between. Closest to the beach are the active and back (primary) dunes that undergo frequent alteration through the effects of the littoral current, spring tides and northeasters. East of Dean Creek, less than half a mile west of Nanny Goat, is a high, wooded ridge of older dunes that are revealed as primary dunes in mid-1920s aerial photographs of the South End—further evidence of the natural accretive effects associated with barrier island sand-sharing.

Salt-spray tolerant vegetation prevalent along the coastal beaches and dunes plays an important role in the ecosystem. Natural plants that proliferate in the active dunes and the back dunes near the beach serve as stabilizers. The most prevalent of these are sea oats (*Uniola paniculata*), which serve as a binder to hold the active dunes in place. Other dune plants serving the same purpose are beach elder, beach hogwort, beach pennywort, water pennywort, beach sand-spur, panic grass, morning glory, and Spanish bayonet (*Yucca*).

In the inter-dune meadow, away from the direct effects of salt, are other stabilizing shrubs and trees, including wax myrtle, red cedar, sand live oak, buckthorn, groundsel, yaupon holly, tamarisk, Muhlenbergia, and prickly pear—a plant that can play havoc with the feet and ankles of unwary strollers through the sand. The dunes and meadow provide feeding habitat and shelter for a variety of animals, especially ghost crabs and rattlesnakes, and a variety of shorebirds.

Tides have a pronounced effect on the shorelines of McIntosh County, including Sapelo Island and the inshore marshes. There is a tidal amplitude around Sapelo ranging about seven feet up to about eleven feet on spring tides. Not surprisingly, the hydraulics of the tides affects the ecology of the marshes to a great extent. Tidal rise and fall is a key factor in the active processes that occur in the marshes, and constitute the diversity of habitats for a number of organisms in the intertidal area. Most tidal creeks lie within steep mud banks and natural levees that create a pattern for the movement of water preceding its eventual dissipation in headwaters on the marsh surface. Tidal waters flow across the low marsh levees only on the highest spring tides. There are two tidal cycles daily with about 600 square miles of marsh and creeks in coastal Georgia being inundated, drained and refilled.[42]

In an ebbtide-dominated regime tidal dynamics are most noticeably pronounced in the waters of the estuarine sounds that provide the breaks between the barrier islands along the coast. By

---

[42] See Albert Sydney Johnson, Hilburn O. Hillestad, Sheryl Fanning Shanholtzer and G. Frederick Shanholtzer, eds., *An Ecological Survey of the Coastal Region of Georgia* (National Park Service Scientific Monograph Series 3, 1974), a useful overview of the ecology of the Georgia coast. The twenty-eight volumes of *Collected Reprints, 1962-2004*, University of Georgia Marine Institute (School of Marine Sciences, Athens), containing the published papers of UGAMI scientists, is the primary source for findings and conclusions based on forty years of scientific field investigations in the salt marsh ecosystem of Sapelo Island and environs. I had frequent interaction with UGAMI scientists while I was manager of the Sapelo Island NERR.

way of example, off Sapelo Island's South End, Doboy Sound has a strong outflow on the ebb tide. This tidal outflow is northwest to southeast. When combined with the input from the nearby Altamaha River, and the north-to-south emergence of water from Old Teakettle Creek, tidal fronts are often quite distinctive, sometimes marked by narrow lines of foam running crossways to the water flow.

Depending on the wind direction, recreational boaters, and even local shrimp boat operators, universally note that Doboy Sound can be some of the roughest water on the Georgia coast. For example, if there is a prevailing southeasterly wind from offshore going against the strong outflow of current from the sound toward the ocean, the waters of the sound can be quite turbulent. The opposite effect prevails if the wind is from the northwest on a flooding tide. Doboy has a slightly lower salinity than the offshore ocean waters due to indirect freshwater inflow from the Altamaha delta just to the south. The Altamaha River system represents one of the largest watersheds in the eastern United States when including the inland Ocmulgee, Oconee and Ohoopee rivers. Substantial amounts of fresh water flow to the sea, mixing with the salt water from the Atlantic in the Altamaha delta just south of Sapelo Island. This brackish mix, occurring up to twenty-five miles inland, affects the hydrology of Doboy Sound, being more pronounced during periods of unusually high flow of fresh water from the interior.

An important component of the tidal interactions within the coastal ecosystem is the phenomena between the barrier islands and the mainland called "dividings." These are areas in which several streams meet and their tidal flows converge—tides meet from different directions and "divide." Most of the barrier islands of Georgia and South Carolina have these convergence areas, dividings, as tidal streams flow though the marshes between the islands and the mainland. Often, changing shoal areas are created at dividings at which the tides flow in different directions. Sandbars shift and the areas of shoaling can create hazards for the unwary mariner. There is one notable area of tidewater McIntosh County where this phenomenon occurs: the Dividings east of Valona is that confluence of several streams where the ebbing and flooding tides meet. If these streams were the points of a compass then Mud River would be to the east, Old Teakettle Creek to the south, Shellbluff Creek from Valona to the west, and the South Sapelo River (Crescent River) to the northwest, all meeting in the middle. Add to these a fifth waterway that has tidal influence, the lower end of Creighton

Narrows just north of the Dividings where it meets the lower end of South Sapelo River.

Mud River, west of Sapelo Island and separating it from the mainland, is aptly named. It is one of coastal Georgia's most distinctive—and unusual—tidal streams. This broad, shallow river was for over a hundred years the principal connection between its confluence with Sapelo Sound on the north and New Teakettle Creek for coasting traffic between Savannah and Darien. It has always been notorious for its difficulty of navigation on anything but high tide, or very nearly high tide. Northeasterly and southwesterly winds (both are prevalent at varying times of the year) tend to practically empty Mud River on an ebbing tide. Much of the mud bottom of the river is exposed at low tide, although locals in anything smaller than a shrimp boat know how to navigate the passage through a narrow channel hugging the marsh. Tides below half-tide are the most unforgiving to those not familiar with local conditions, for the mud bottom can't be seen, yet is only a foot or less below the surface. There are numerous examples of the problems encountered with this waterway. The following account, written by a coastal traveler in 1853, is typical:

"...We passed through sounds and creeks and narrow rivers, some so narrow and shallow that two steamboats cannot pass each other, and not infrequently, the boats ground, lying in the mud over one tide. When they get fast to the soft bottom, all efforts of course are made to get them off, the most effectual being to send a boat ahead, manned by half a dozen negroes who, taking a stout rope with them, fasten it to a long pole thrust deeply down into the soft mud in a slanting position, and then attach the other end of the rope to the capstan on board the steamer; that, turned by the aid of the engines, soon drags them out of the mud. We grounded in the Mud River at half tide. For some miles the tide went out and left us high and dry as if we had been in the middle of a prairie. I tried to see for myself how far I could thrust a pole into the mud, and taking one about 20 feet long, I forced it down by my own strength from 12 to 15 feet. We were released when the water returned to half tide, and went on our way rejoicing. I truly said that this route was a novel one. Now we would be shut into a narrow stream and then we would come out again almost into the open sea..."[43]

The situation was finally rectified in 1913 with the Corps of Engineers dredging a cut, Creighton Narrows, through the marsh

---

[43] Joseph W. Smith, *Visits to Brunswick, Georgia and Travels South* (Boston, 1907), 18-19.

connecting the Dividings with Front River, thus enabling marine traffic to bypass Mud River altogether.[44]

Perhaps the best example of a tidal waterway and its interaction with, and influence by, tidal cycles is the Duplin River which flows within Sapelo Island. The Duplin, largest of the streams lying entirely within the marshes of Sapelo, transits the western side of the island, emptying on its Southern end into Doboy Sound. Except for rainfall and groundwater discharge from the nearby uplands, the Duplin receives no freshwater, and thus can be more accurately defined as a large tidal creek or embayment. Along its six-and-a-half mile length, the Duplin has three distinct sections, or tidal "prisms." The lower component ends near Pumpkin Hammock, the second extends northward to Moses Hammock, and the third comprises the several tidal creek branches of the upper Duplin.

The strong tidal currents and the lack of freshwater input generally keep the hydrological dynamics of the upper Duplin excluded from those of the lower section of the river nearer Doboy Sound. Occasionally, during especially high spring tides, water in the upper Duplin may merge with that of Mud River a short distance to the north. Conversely, the lower Duplin can sometimes have lower salinity levels than that of the upper sections during times of heavy discharge from the Altamaha River into Doboy Sound. The Duplin estuary covers 3,300 acres, about fifteen per cent of which remains submerged at mean low water with a tidal excursion of about three miles.[45]

A survey of the Duplin by University of Georgia Marine Institute scientists in the 1950s determined that the river's water surface was relatively narrow at low tide. When the water rises to six feet above mean low tide, however, it begins to leave the banks and flow in a sheet across the marsh. Small increases in tidal height impel increased volumes of water into the estuary, and as a consequence the tidal flow is turbulent. This promotes greater turbidity, though marsh flushing is incomplete with very little fresh water entering the system. Most water in the estuary merely oscillates back and forth, rather than draining away to be replaced. The sediments in the bed of the Duplin are low in mud content and contain accumulations of

---

[44] The development of the Atlantic Intracoastal Waterway in McIntosh County, with its attendant dredging operations, is covered in Buddy Sullivan, *Early Days on the Georgia Tidewater*, all editions, 1990-2018.
[45] Johnson, Hillestad, et.al., *Ecological Survey of the Coastal Region of Georgia*, 91.

Creighton Island, north end: a good example of the transition of the tidal salt marsh to upland.

shell material, much of which is deposited from the oyster banks along the river. At Little Sapelo Island and Pumpkin Hammock the river is eroding sandy Pleistocene deposits.[46]

The intertidal habitat of the Duplin, and its largest tributary, Barn Creek, is teeming with marine organisms that receive nutrients from the marshes, and in turn, provide food sources for saltwater fish species. The Marine Institute has conducted much of its research in these marshes, and over the last half century has made important discoveries relative to the feeding habits of subtidal species. Microalgae are productive in the river, and these and other organisms provide a food source for juvenile menhaden, a plankton feeder. Menhaden, in turn, are preyed upon by larger fish and birds. Flounder, bluefish and yellowtail are other finfish predators in the estuary; mullet are deposit feeders, and mummichog live in the shallower creeks and headwaters where they are rarely threatened by larger fish. Shrimp utilize the creeks off the Duplin throughout the year, and are especially prevalent during the summer. Larger predators, such as dolphins that feed around Marsh Landing dock on the lower Duplin, and mink and otter forage in the smaller creeks

[46] R.G. Wiegert and B.J. Freeman, *Tidal Salt Marshes of the Southeast Atlantic Coast: A Community Profile* (Washington, DC: U.S. Department of the Interior, Fish and Wildlife Service, 1990); R.A. Ragotzkie and R.A. Bryson, "Hydrography of the Duplin River, Sapelo Island, Georgia," *Bulletin of Marine Science of the Gulf and Caribbean* 5 (1955): 297-314.

and marsh edges; birds feed in the tidal waters as well—pelicans, gulls and terns nearer the sound, and blue herons, ospreys and egrets further up the Duplin.

Eugene P. Odum, ecologist of the University of Georgia, and regarded as the "father of modern ecology," once described tidal creeks as a great circulatory system driven by the pumping "heart" of the tides. Tidal creeks and smaller rivers provide new water input to the marshes on each high tide, while flushing out and removing many of the by-products of marsh growth and marsh decay—detritus—on the ebbing tide. Some of the creeks are almost bare at low tide leaving exposed mud banks that serve as habitat to a variety of consumers such as fiddler crabs, herons, egrets, and marsh hens. On a flooding tide, snails become active while periwinkles and insects graze on the stems of the marsh cordgrass. Plankton and juveniles of various species enter the creeks with incoming tides, as do shrimp and fish when the water becomes deep enough.

McIntosh County's salt marshes are composed of many plant species, but the most prevalent by far is smooth cordgrass—*Spartina alterniflora*—which comprises about ninety per cent of the marsh system, and receives the greatest amount of tidal inundation. Despite its low diversity the marsh is considered to be one of the most productive natural areas on earth.[47] The basis for the marsh food chain is detritus originating from the dominant vascular plant, the cordgrass. There are differences in the *Spartina* along the creek banks, and that of the high marsh nearer the transitional zone that is comprised of a mix of short *Spartina*, and *Salicornia* marsh. Low marsh *Spartina* is taller and more luxuriant than other marshes, and prevails along the creek and river fringes. All life requires fresh water to carry on metabolic processes, and the marshes have unique mechanisms that allow them to extract fresh water from the saline waters of the estuary.[48]

[47] E.P. Odum and C.L. Schelske, "Mechanisms Maintaining High Productivity in Georgia Estuaries," *Proceedings* of the Gulf and Caribbean Fish Institute 14 (1961): 75-80.

[48] The most lucid study of the *Spartina* marsh ecosystem, minus the technical jargon, is Charles Seabrook, *The World of the Salt Marsh: Appreciating and Protecting the Tidal Marshes of the Southeastern Atlantic Coast* (Athens: University of Georgia Press, 2012). See also Mildred Teal and John Teal, *Portrait of an Island* (New York: Atheneum, 1964) and Teal and Teal, *Life and Death of a Salt Marsh* (New York: Atlantic, 1969).

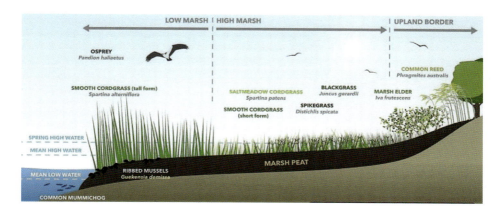

Marsh soils are anaerobic except near the surface and around the roots. Soil bacteria that breaks down accumulated organic matter require an anaerobic environment with the rate of breakdown, and that in which plant nutrients become available for new marsh growth, being related to water-flow characteristics and the dispersal of waste products.[49] Plant zonation is always subject to elevation and hydrology but there is a water table that maintains the marsh sediments in a near waterlogged state in all but the highest intertidal elevations.[50] Consequently, there is a high diversity of plant, soil, and microbial attributes between the low and high *Spartina* zones.

Salt marsh requires nitrogen and phosphorus as nutrients, the latter of which is abundantly available in both the soil and the tidal waters. Nitrogen availability is more complicated. The use of this common air element by *Spartina* requires its conversion to ammonia, nitrate or nitrite by the marsh through blue-green algae on the marsh surface, and bacteria within the soil.[51] Thus, the adaptability of the marsh to natural processes in a salt water environment makes it one of the more unique plant species of any ecosystem.

Twice-daily tidal cycles convey nutrients into the marshes, export detritus and nutrients back into the estuary, and provide a large

[49] J.R. Wadsworth, "Geomorphic Characteristics of Tidal Drainage Networks in the Duplin River System, Sapelo Island, Georgia," PhD diss., University of Georgia, 1980; R.W. Frey and P. Basan, "Coastal Salt Marshes," in R.A. Davis, Jr., ed. *Coastal Sedimentary Environments*, 2nd edit. (New York: Springer-Verlag, 1985), 225-301.
[50] Wiegert and Freeman, *Tidal Salt Marshes of the Southeast Atlantic Coast.* See also the many technical papers relating to marsh studies in *Collected Reprints*, UGAMI.
[51] L.R. Pomeroy and R.G. Wiegert, *The Ecology of a Salt Marsh* (New York: Springer-Verlag, 1981).

surface area for phytoplankton production. Tidal flushing maintains a desirable vertical distribution of nutrients and detritus; the base of the detritus food chain is decayed *Spartina*, which is attacked by microorganisms.

Marine Institute research has determined that bacteria found in Sapelo's marsh mud are an important link in the food chain. In the late 1950s, John Teal found the important detritus-algae feeders to be fiddler crabs, periwinkle snails and nematodes among Sapelo's deposit feeders. The utilization of marsh organic matter accounts for about fifty-five per cent of production, leaving about forty-five per cent available for support of finfish, crabs, shrimp, oysters, and other estuarine species.[52] Further investigations found that marsh algae form a thin stratum between a dark, nutrient-rich, anaerobic sediment, and either an illuminated, aerobic, comparatively nutrient-poor water column. Thus, the algae habitat is subjected to rapid changes in light, temperature, pH, salinity, and nutrients that can have correspondingly rapid effects on the photosynthetic rate. Benthic productivity was found to represent about twelve per cent of the net primary production of the macrophytes in the marsh. About seventy-five per cent of this production occurs during ebbing tides, with the exposed creek banks being the most productive areas.[53]

In the higher intertidal zone between the *Spartina* and the upland, areas subjected to less frequent tidal inundation, other marsh-type plants are prevalent. Glasswort and saltgrass appear mixed with the shorter cordgrass. Black needlerush (*Juncus roemerianus*) develops as patches amid the cordgrass with its thin grey-brown stalks and sharp points. Other salt-tolerant plants mixed with the short *Spartina* in this zone are marsh bulrush and sea oxeye. Also featured in the higher zones are salt pans—barren sections of flat, packed soil that is free of vegetation because of its excessively high salinity.

Areas of vegetation lying amid *Spartina* marsh along the fringe abutting a tidal creek, or even a short distance apart from the uplands, are clumps of vegetation of varying size known as hammocks. These formations of high ground feature a mix of similar vegetation, including red cedar, sabal palm, wax myrtle, and yaupon

---

[52] John M. Teal, "Energy Flow in the Salt Marsh Ecosystem of Georgia," *Ecology* 43 (1962): 614-24.

[53] L.R. Pomeroy, W.M. Darley, E.L. Dunn, J.L. Gallagher, E.B. Haines and D.M. Whitney, "Primary Production," in Pomeroy and Wiegert, *Ecology of a Salt Marsh*, 39-67.

Low marsh and transition zone to myrtle, glasswort and palm.

holly. Hammock characteristics are similar, and they range in size
from less than an acre to several acres. Many coastal hammocks have
Pleistocene bases surrounded by their Holocene marshes. Other
hammocks are more recent, being comprised of dredge spoil
deposited on the marsh banks with the development of vegetation

increasing with the passage of time, primarily red cedar, scrub oak, sabal palm and wax myrtle.

A variety of marine organisms utilize the marshes for nutrients as decomposing *Spartina* detritus gradually dissolves and is flushed by the tides to provide food. Numerous consumer species inhabit the marsh ecosystem with the major groups being comprised of zooplankton, benthic invertebrates, insects, fishes, reptiles, birds and mammals. Benthic macro-invertebrates are the most conspicuous of the consumers, particularly fiddler crabs (*Uca* species), marsh mussel (*Geukensia demissa*), and marsh periwinkle (*Littorino irrorata*). Noticeable along some creek banks are oyster reefs. Oysters (*Crassostrea virginica*) settle on solid surfaces along the banks and subtidal water; as filter feeders they use marsh nutrients as an important food source. Oyster beds can alter tidal flow in the creeks by creating pools and small breakwaters. In the early decades of the twentieth century, Georgia salt marshes supported a sizeable oyster industry but over-exploitation, and the failure to replace shell, led to its near-collapse by the 1950s. Another beneficiary of marsh nutrients directly related to commercial use is the Atlantic blue crab (*Callinectus sapidus*), the majority of which are taken in the sounds and the smaller rivers and creeks. Crabs use the marshes and creeks as habitat during their juvenile and sub-adult stages.

Of even greater economic significance, the marsh is critical in supporting the coastal shrimp fishery, long a multi-million-dollar industry on the Georgia coast, with peak production in the middle decades of the twentieth century. While coastal shrimp (*Penaeus*) spawn in the open ocean, they migrate to the inshore waters as juveniles, and depend on marsh-produced nutrients during their growth stages before returning to the sea.

At low tide, the ubiquitous fiddler crab, particularly the sand fiddler (*Uca pugilator*), is frequently observed scuttling along the mudflats foraging for food near its burrow. Fiddlers extract food from the substrate based on differing feeding stimulants in response to levels in the food resource.[54] Gradients in biotic and abiotic factors resulting from tidal flooding affect the distribution of marsh organisms with the structural characteristics of *Spartina* providing refuge for some species from predators and submergence. The

---

[54] J.R. Robertson, K. Bancroft, G. Vermeer, and K. Plaiser, "Experimental Studies on the Foraging Behavior of the Sand Fiddler Crab," *Journal of Experimental Marine Biology and Ecology* 52 (1980): 47-64.

periwinkle prevalent in the marshes is a favorite of predators, particularly the blue crab.

Much of the current understanding of the salt marsh ecosystem and its attendant rivers, creeks and dividings, and the biological and chemical processes that occur within these systems, began to be formulated after 1953 with the establishment of the University of Georgia Marine Institute on Sapelo Island. A young biology professor at the University of Georgia, Eugene P. Odum (1913-2002), who was laying the foundation for the first serious investigations of saltmarsh ecosystems on the southeastern coast, and several of his colleagues, worked with Sapelo owner Richard J. Reynolds, Jr. to make it possible for the marine biological laboratory to come to Sapelo.[55]

Ecological research in the first forty years often entailed field studies stemming from two basic considerations: determining the water flow characteristics of *Spartina alterniflora* (smooth cordgrass marsh), and the chemical and biological processes associated with *Spartina*, in concert with the marine organisms that proliferate the marsh ecosystem, or are directly affected by the marsh. Eventually, an important connection was made between the dynamics of the natural processes occurring in the salt marshes, and the sustainability of marine life in the nearshore and estuarine waters, as Emory Thomas points out:

"This transmittal through tidal action of organic matter is primarily in the form of detritus which is mostly decomposed *Spartina*. The process by which detritus enters the ocean is called 'outwelling' and the initial hypothesis among Odum and the other scientists at the University of Georgia Marine Institute was that this outwelling from salt marshes and estuaries lay at the base of the food chain which supported the abundant marine life found off the east coast. Thus there seemed to be an empirical connection between *Spartina* and shrimp cocktail at least. In very recent years, however, scientists have challenged the assumption that 'outwelling' from salt marshes is vital to the food chain in coastal waters."[56]

---

[55] Betty Jean Craige, *Eugene Odum: Ecosystem Ecologist & Environmentalist* (Athens: University of Georgia Press, 2001). 54-58. An overview of the first forty years of research at the UGA Marine Institute is found in Buddy Sullivan, *Sapelo, People and Place on a Georgia Sea Island* (Athens: University of Georgia Press, 2017).

[56] Emory M. Thomas, "The South and the Sea: Some Thoughts on the Southern Maritime Tradition," *Georgia Historical Quarterly* 67 (Summer 1983).

Tidal creek and low marsh, Barn Creek, Sapelo Island, looking west toward Little Sapelo Island.

Odum's research in those early years at Sapelo had important ramifications for the work of the Marine Institute in its first two decades. It also influenced his own evolving attitudes about ecology and environmentalism. Odum expresses an almost spiritual connection to the marsh and tides:

"We moved up tidal creeks in small outboard motor boats on ebbing tides; we found ourselves in deep canyons of golden mud banks, topped by six-foot high stands of marsh grass looking for all the world like a well-fertilized stand of sugar cane. The notion came to us in those early days that we were in the arteries of a remarkable energy-absorbing natural system whose heart was the pumping action of the tides. The entire tideland complex of barrier islands, marshes, creeks, and river mouths was a single operational unit linked together by the tide. If we were right, each part of the system would have to be dependent for its life-sustaining energy not only on the direct rays of the sun, but also on the energy of the tides...Does nature routinely exploit tidal power as men have dreamed of doing for centuries? In the past, biologists who studied estuarine and seashore organisms had been preoccupied with how such life adapts to the obvious stresses; that some of the stresses might be converted to subsidies was, and still is, something of a new theory. This germ of an idea, subsequently developed by twenty years of team research on Sapelo, will, we hope, provide the basis for man to design with, rather than against, nature on this remarkable sea coast."[57]

---

[57] Eugene P. Odum, "Living Marsh," in Robert Hanie, *Guale: The Golden Coast of Georgia* (San Francisco: Friends of the Earth, 1974), Introduction.

An understanding of the influence of tidal salt marsh ecosystems in the southeastern United States began to manifest itself as early as the 1890s, based on government surveys and research. These reviews provided a basis for the significant ecological research that began fifty years later. In 1889, the Georgia legislature began framing regulations and guidelines for commercial oyster harvesting on the coast; the state requested federal assistance in gathering data to guide state authorities in devising laws for the developing industry. What resulted was a report by J.C. Drake, Ensign, U.S. Navy, who in 1889 conducted field investigations with scientists along the Georgia coast, which revealed extensive intertidal and subtidal oyster beds in areas of the tidewater. He also consulted local oystermen who were familiar with local waters and the characteristics of the oyster beds therein. In his conclusions, Drake noted that the natural oyster beds of Georgia had been depleted by excessive fishing without replenishment of the beds in harvested areas. He noted:

"...The recent oyster law of the State does not require a knowledge of the location and area of the natural beds. It very properly permits anyone to enter grounds for private cultivation on any oyster bed which is not reported to by the public for the procuring of oysters by the use of tongs for consumption or for sale. So dew and so small are the oysters which now remain scattered along the shores that it would be to the interest of the State if its citizens were permitted to lease any area, the State selling to the highest bidder the now almost depleted oyster beds. As a means of rapidly depleting the natural beds no more effective method could be instituted than the establishment of factories for the canning of oysters. These in the end will be of great benefit to the State, because the sooner the natural beds are depleted the sooner will the citizens engage in private cultivation, and enact laws that will give inducement to capital."[58]

McIntosh County, indeed much of coastal Georgia and South Carolina, had productive oyster harvests in the late nineteenth and early twentieth centuries. However, as Drake observed, overfishing the resource without proper follow-on conservation—replenishment of the resource—ultimately led to a decline in the fishery. "As early as 1889, Drake noted a general depletion of oyster beds, especially beds

[58] J.C. Drake, "On the Sounds and Estuaries of Georgia with Reference to Oyster Culture," U.S. Coast and Geodetic Survey, Bulletin No. 19, March 1890, 201.

OYSTER FACTORY AND SUMMER RESORT.   VALONA, GA.

Oyster cannery and boats on Shellbluff Creek, Valona, ca. 1906.

which were located near oyster houses," one study pointed out. "Drake felt that continued depletion, especially that which was expected as a result of cannery harvest, would ultimately be beneficial to the industry by forcing private cultivation and the enactment of reasonable transplanting laws."[59]

Drake's advice went largely unheeded, despite new regulations in the Georgia Code after 1889 by which commercial oyster harvesters were required to return a portion of the shells harvested to the growing area. "Judging from Drake's report, Georgia's oyster laws were difficult to enforce, as they are today. Failure to replace shell material to harvested areas is probably the most significant reason for the depletion of Georgia's oyster resources."[60] These lessons had not been learned a generation later. By 1950 the Georgia industry was in great decline with harvests well below those of the more productive years of the early 1900s. Subtidal and intertidal oysters were raked from the river and creek banks, and bottoms with little or no re-seeding, causing a reduction in spat, hence far fewer adult oysters were available for harvest as time went along. Disease virtually wiped out what remained of the industry in Georgia and South Carolina during the 1970s and 80s.

Similar ecological applications are pertinent to the coastal shrimp fishery that began in earnest in the early twentieth century. Much of the understanding of the life cycle of the shrimp, and its relevance to

---

[59] C. Duane Harris, "Survey of the Intertidal and Subtidal Oyster Resources of the Georgia Coast," Coastal Resources Division, GDNR, 1980, 5.
[60] Ibid., 10.

164

the salt marsh ecosystem, evolved from the 1950s and 1960s research at the Marine Institute on Sapelo Island.

The salt marshes and estuarine waters of coastal Georgia serve as a nursery ground for the *penaid* shrimp that prevail along the southeastern coast. Adults breed in the deeper offshore waters where about a million eggs are released by each female. The eggs hatch into tiny young shrimp that bear no resemblance to their parents. These larval shrimp float to the surface and are carried inshore by the currents. En route they undergo additional transformation in body form, and when they reach the beaches, sounds, rivers and creeks inshore of the islands, they settle to the bottom looking more like the adult shrimp they will become. The juvenile shrimp mature in the creeks and rivers, being sustained by the nutrients of the decaying marshes flushed out by the tides. In less than a year the shrimp move back into the open sea to spawn and begin another life cycle.

This shrimp cycle, and its reliance on the marsh ecosystem for nutrients only came to be understood through the research of estuarine scientists conducting field research at the University of Georgia Marine Institute on Sapelo Island, and at similar research centers on the southeast coast. Their findings relating to the life cycle of shrimp, and its inter-relationship with the marsh ecosystem, assumed great importance by the late 1960s. Over the years, the Georgia inshore sounds were gradually scoured of young white shrimp. This attrition meant that fewer mature shrimp were returning to Atlantic offshore waters to spawn. In 1970 the Georgia General Assembly passed an important piece of environmental legislation with enactment of the Marshlands Protection Act, which not only implemented protective measures to conserve the state's marsh ecosystem, but also permanently closed the coastal sounds to commercial shrimp trawling. Offshore trawling near the beaches was permitted only at certain times of the year. Otherwise the boats had to fish in deeper waters. As a result, the shrimp population gradually began to replenish itself but by then, the future of the southeast shrimping industry was in trouble due to a variety of other factors. For example, the 1974 Arab oil embargo and the consequent shortages, as well as the precipitous rise in the cost of diesel fuel, hurt the fishery. Profits were reduced, and by the late 1970s and early 1980s many career shrimpers had left the industry. Successive severe winters from 1983-86 damaged the shrimp crop due to much colder waters than normal. Finally, the increasing importation of foreign-

Floyd Atwood on his shrimp boat, Cedar Creek, mid-1940s.

cultivated shrimp undercut the U.S. domestic market causing more fishermen to seek other livelihoods.

By 1930, the McIntosh shrimp fishery was well-established. A government survey compiled the year before noted: "A large and varied industry of McIntosh County is the gathering, preparation and sale of seafood. Approximately 40,000 cases of shrimp, worth about $200,000, and 15,000 cases of oysters, worth about $75,000, are canned and shipped annually; in addition, about 2,000 barrels of fresh, or 'green', shrimp worth about $75,000, are also shipped. Most of the canned shrimp is shipped to the New England states and the oysters are utilized mostly in the Southeastern states."[61] After World War II, the fishery further expanded through technological advances and improved techniques in trawler construction. Trawlers were larger and as a consequence, were able to venture forth from the coastal sounds into the open sea to drag for shrimp.

Ice-making was an important factor in the growth of the fishery in the mid-to-late 1940s. It was about that time that Guy H. Amason came to Cedar Point and developed an ice manufacturing plant that

---

[61] *Soil Survey of McIntosh County* (Series 1929), U.S. Department of Agriculture, Bureau of Chemistry and Soils, Washington, D.C., 1932.

provided an immediate lift to the local fishery. Boats could now take on ice to preserve their catches, and thus remain at sea for longer periods of time, trawling for more shrimp when they were "running" as well as conserving fuel by reducing runs back to port. Amason also owned several boats and marketed his own shrimp, and that of others locally, at his Amason Enterprises.

Until the mid-1940s most shrimpers had to haul their nets in by hand using thick manila rope. After the Second World War several innovations emerged to more efficiently facilitate the dragging and recovery of nets, such as powered winches and steel cable. Another technological development was the double-outrigger. By the early 1960s, all of the larger boats were being fitted with double trawl booms to enable them to drag two nets simultaneously rather than one. Like ice-making, these improvements enabled the shrimp fishery to prosper. Also, starting in the 1940s, truck lines began to develop, many being operated primarily for the rapid transport of iced-down boxes of shrimp direct from the docks to processors in Georgia and Florida.

The early 1950s to the mid-1970s was the peak era for the commercial fishery at Cedar Point and Valona, indeed for all of McIntosh County. In 1960 there were thirty-five trawlers home-ported at Valona, twenty-eight at Darien, and twenty-four at Cedar Point.[62] By 1995 there were third-and-fourth generation shrimpers in McIntosh County. By then, however, it was difficult to consistently prosper in the industry due to the rising costs of fuel, maintenance, and marine insurance (for those who could afford it), and worst of all, the preponderance of imported shrimp from distant countries which undercut the domestic markets on the south Atlantic and Gulf coasts. In 2020, the industry was a shadow of its former self, demonstrated most vividly by the weight of numbers: Georgia shrimp landings of 16 million pounds in 1960, one of the peak years, were down to 2 million pounds in 2003; and the number of licensed trawlers in Georgia, from a high of 1,500 boats in 1978, was down to only 246 in 2013, the lowest number of vessels operating since the 1920s.[63]

---

[62] List compiled by the author ca. 1961, in author's personal collection, with the names of the vessels, their owners, and their home port.
[63] Records of annual shrimp landings and boat registrations, Coastal Resources Division, GDNR, Brunswick, Ga.

The upland wooded areas contiguous to the marshes on the McIntosh County mainland, as well as areas of Sapelo Island and Blackbeard islands, are characterized by a mixed maritime forest dominated by stands of mature live oak (*Quercus virginiana*), and several varieties of pine (*Pinus*). Other sections of the upland forest comprise a mixed oak-hardwood community, but with less presence of pine. Here there are live oak, laurel oak, water oak, hickory, bay, holly, magnolia, and some slash pine. The oaks with their low, spreading limbs support various vines and epiphytes (air plants), the latter dominated by Spanish moss and resurrection fern. The latter epiphyte appears dead and dried out in its dormant phase but springs to life, lush and green, during periods of rainfall. Wending their way around the gnarled thick lower trunks and limbs of the oaks are grapevines and Virginia creeper. Spanish moss is a bromeliad and features tiny green flowers, hardly visible. Moss is a distinctive feature of the oaks but can also be observed on other tree species. Often seen on or near the marsh fringes are stands of native cabbage palm (*Sabal palmetto*) with an understory dominated by wax myrtle, broomsedge and panic grass in uncleared areas.

Along McIntosh County's tidal areas and on the larger islands, there are several distinct ecologies and forest zones: upland hardwood maritime forests, lowland hardwood forests, old and new pine plantations, and grassy savannahs. The lowland forests are typically found in wetter areas, and are comprised of live oak, water oak, loblolly pine, hickory, blackgum, sweetgum, and sweetbay, set amidst thick understorys of palmetto and wax myrtle.

Proper timber management, both on the McIntosh County mainland by the timber corporations, and on Sapelo by the state, provides open food habitat for deer and other species, and facilitates the healthy growth of the maritime forest and commercial pine plantations. Mixed stands of oak and pine are scattered in many areas of the county's uplands, with closed oak canopies beneath many of the pines. The selective cutting of pine by the state and private entities usually results in cleared habitat for deer herds, and has hastened the regeneration of natural oak and other hardwood species in parts of the timbered areas. Large sections of the maritime forest on the McIntosh mainland and the larger islands are dominated by pine-palmetto vegetation with the pine canopy rarely closed. Though pine is cut selectively, natural seeding remains effective in some areas. Saw palmetto form dense thickets four to five feet tall amid the pine forests and is often interspersed with other vegetation.

In a number of areas along highway 99 in McIntosh County near the coast between Meridian and Eulonia, and on either side of the road from South Newport to Harris Neck, will be observed cleared, grassy meadows, some being open grasslands, or savannahs, usually the result of manmade modifications for agriculture and cattle pasturage in the nineteenth and early twentieth centuries. On Sapelo Island a good example is King Savannah, which has thick stands of bahia grass (*Poaceae notatum*) planted earlier as forage for cattle herds. While a much smaller tract than Sapelo, the same applies to Creighton Island where open pasture lands and savannahs on both the south end and north end can be observed. Many areas of the islands and the eastern mainland tidewater are clear and open, evidence of earlier crop cultivation.

One of the best means of exemplifying the connectedness of ecology and land use in McIntosh County is through a review of its soil types, particularly in areas of the county that will come under scrutiny in future chapters of this study. The soils of Sapelo and Creighton islands and other tidewater sections of the county, such as Harris Neck and west along the South Newport River, Sutherland's Bluff and other Sapelo River tracts, and areas along either side of highway 99 from Crescent to just north of Darien, are derived primarily from quartz sands. These generally have high permeability, a condition that results in low water-holding capacity and rapid leaching. These soils range from deep, well-drained sands to poorly drained thick black loam surfaces and subsurface horizons of gray sands. Most of the soils, however, range from moderately well-drained to poorly-drained. These coastal soils are generally highly acidic, whether they are well-drained or poorly-drained. According to the most recent soil survey of McIntosh County (1959), the pH of the soil in the county's tidewater areas range from 4.1 to 7.4 among the twelve identified soil types inventoried. Additionally, nineteenth and early-to-mid- twentieth century agriculture and cattle operations resulted in the clearing, ditching, and draining of many upland areas, thus altering both the natural hydrology as well as the soil dynamics in some areas. This is particularly true of parts of Sapelo Island, the Altamaha delta bottomlands and large areas of the western sections of McIntosh County, which is dominated by low-lying swamps and forested timber land.[64]

Hydrological factors especially come into play in McIntosh County's eastern tidewater areas, including the islands. On the beaches of Sapelo, Blackbeard and Wolf islands, high salt concentrations in dune sands inhibit the vertical percolation of rainwater through the dunes. This limited water supply reduces the amount of vegetation on the seaward side of the county's islands. On the inshore islands, the western sides of the larger barrier islands, and along the eastern mainland tidewater the salts exert an influence on vegetation in the intertidal zone between the marshes and the upland, and tend to limit species diversity. The abundant nutrients, however, enable the relatively few species in these areas to be highly productive. Conversely, there are hard salt pans in the high marsh in some areas that are so concentrated in salts, usually two or more times that of sea water, that few vascular plants can grow there. Good examples are seen along the Valona road on the mainland and near Dean Creek on the South End of Sapelo.

The tidal marshes are non-cultivable but are sufficiently above the frequent influence of tidal inundation to allow vegetation of red cedar, small oaks and coarse grasses. These areas include the marsh zones of the smaller islands, such as Creighton and Little Sapelo, where tidal inundation occasionally occurs, and on the eastern shore of the mainland along the coast from the South Newport River, Harris Neck, lower Bruro Neck, White Chimney, and from Belleville southward to the Darien River, including areas around Baisden's Bluff, Cedar Point, Valona, Hudson, the Thicket, the Ridge and the marsh islands of Hird, Black and Mayhall. Soils identified as High tidal marsh, and subject to more frequent periods of tidal inundation, such as on spring tides, fringe the upland marsh transition zones and have vegetation of wax myrtle, marsh elder, saltwort and sea oxeye. Low tidal marsh is comprised almost exclusively of smooth cordgrass (*Spartina*) with pockets of black needlerush (*Juncus*) in the higher areas. The prevailing soil on the seaward sides of the barrier islands is Coastal beach sand, a wide strip that runs along the entire easternmost edge of McIntosh County, including Blackbeard and Cabretta islands, Nanny Goat Beach on Sapelo Island's South End, and Wolf Island. Strips of porous

---

[64] Hubert J. Byrd, D.G. Aydelott, et. al., *Soil Survey of McIntosh County, Georgia*, Series 1959 (Washington, DC: U.S. Department of Agriculture, 1961). The discussion here is based on the 1959 survey.

Blanton and Lakeland sands are featured on the upland sand ridges on both the north and south ends of Blackbeard Island. However, on a sand ridge in Blackbeard's northwest corner there is a strip of Palm Beach fine sand, validating the use of that small section of the island for cotton cultivation in the early 1800s.

There are two other areas of McIntosh County that should be mentioned for their soil types. In the Altamaha delta the only soil is that identified as Wet Alluvial land, found nowhere else in the county. In an earlier 1929 soil survey this rich bottomland was labeled as Altamaha clay. It includes the western part of Broughton Island, all of Champneys, Butler's, Cambers, Generals and Carr's islands, the western half of Rhett's Island, and along both sides of Cathead Creek to about three miles west of Darien. These were all areas of rice cultivation in the nineteenth century. The other area is the western section of the county which is largely comprised of soils labeled as Swamp, in addition to the Bladen series of sands and clays, which are not conducive to large-scale agriculture such as that practiced in the Altamaha bottomlands, the coastal islands and the county's eastern tidewater. Much of the western part of the county is comprised of large swampy areas, along with drier sandy areas commonly called the pine flatwoods. One interesting soil type stands out from the others mentioned here, that being Lakeland coarse sand. It is prevalent in only two areas of McIntosh County, one being an extensive strip in the southwest section of the county immediately north of Buffalo Swamp, running west to the Long County line. It is an area known as the "sand hills," part of which touch on the Altamaha River at Fort Barrington and Barrington and Harper's lakes, and at Possum Point at the headwaters of Lewis Creek. The only other area Lakeland sand is found in the county is on the sand ridges of Blackbeard Island.

Relevant to the forgoing discussion it must be kept in mind that sizeable sections of McIntosh County have been subjected to modification of varying degrees by human activity over the last two-and-a-half centuries, primarily for agriculture, cattle-herding, and timbering. Successive private owners in areas of the county and on the islands constructed irrigation canals and ditches to drain off low-lying sections, particularly in the Altamaha delta and on Sapelo Island, and built levees and embankments to facilitate agriculture and timbering. Irrigation ditches were dug by slave labor in the nineteenth century to facilitate crop production and the watering of livestock. Some of the nineteenth century ditches on Sapelo Island were improved and enlarged in the 1920s through dynamiting operations during H.E. Coffin's ownership. Evidence of the ditches made or enlarged with dynamite is conspicuous in places on the south and central portions of Sapelo. Pursuant to modifications for truck farming, there was also ditching on Butler's and Champneys islands in the 1930s and 1940s to improve drainage provided by earlier irrigation ditches associated with nineteenth century rice planting.

About one third of McIntosh County is salt marsh, islands, marsh hammocks and a complex network of sounds, tidal rivers and creeks, some of which penetrate well inland, such as the South Newport and Sapelo rivers. From the beginning of the county's English settlement, human populations have tended to inhabit upland tracts on or near the rivers and creeks—areas such as South Newport, Priester, Harris Neck, Shellman Bluff, Sutherland's Bluff, Belleville, Pine Harbor, Baisden's Bluff, Cedar Point, Valona, Hudson, the Thicket, Ridgeville and Darien. These areas of the coast are largely drained by Sapelo and Doboy sounds, the South Newport and Sapelo rivers, the tidal tributaries attached thereto, and the freshwater-influenced Altamaha River and its estuary.

West of the tidewater is an altogether different ecosystem, particularly with respect to that section west of U.S. highway 17. Compared to the tidewater, the western half of the county is very sparsely populated. Here there are fresh-water swamps, pine flatwoods, palmetto thickets, pockets of sand hill ridges, and open meadows that once served as cattle pasturage. The larger swamps are occasionally flooded by seasonal spring freshets from the Altamaha, and consequently are regarded as some of the most inaccessible areas of McIntosh County. The largest are Buffalo Swamp on the south, drained by the Altamaha River, Lewis Creek and Cathead Creek, Young's Swamp in the central part of the county, Big Mortar and Oscar swamps in the western section and Bull Town Swamp between McIntosh and Liberty counties, drained by the South Newport River.

The ecological dynamic of the Altamaha delta is vastly different from that of the tidewater and pine flatwoods. The delta is an area that, prior to English settlement, was dominated by dense cypress hardwood swamps and other wetlands. After the Revolution the cypress swamps in the lower Altamaha gave way to large-scale rice production with planters utilizing the soils of the rich river bottomlands washed down to the coast from middle Georgia. Here the nineteenth century planters produced rice as a money staple, with cotton and sugar cane as rotation crops. These areas are unpopulated now, being under state administration as protected waterfowl management areas.

Animal species common to the McIntosh islands and tidewater areas are white-tailed deer, raccoons, opossum, squirrels, otters, minks, armadillos, and feral hogs and cattle. Eastern diamondback rattlesnakes populate the uplands and beach dunes, cottonmouth water moccasins are in the wetter areas, and numerous species of non-venomous snakes are commonly encountered in the less-cleared areas. It is likely that much, perhaps most, of the flora and fauna encountered today is not the same as that of the Archaic period (10,000-3,000 B.P.). During the Archaic most of the area was covered by a climax forest, which would have reduced the available food supply in the spring and summer. There would have been browsing areas available in the shrub-herb layers of the ecosystem but it would not have supported the large deer herds, and other wildlife that prevail today with open pastures and second-and-third generation forest growth. As oak species matured in the Archaic, the fall and winter months would have produced sufficient acorn fall to support deer in greater numbers as time went along; Spanish moss and plants growing in the high marsh would have provided additional food sources. The remaining vestiges of the maritime climax forest from that period disappeared when large areas of the islands and coastal mainland were cleared for agriculture and oak timbering in the eighteenth and nineteenth centuries. If the early climax forest was not seriously depleted during the proto-historic and aboriginal agricultural eras, then it almost certainly was during the colonial period and after.

Weather is an important component of local environmental considerations. McIntosh County's climate is classified as sub-tropical, consisting of brief, relatively mild winters, and warm, humid summers. Cold temperatures in some winters prevent tropical or sub-tropical vegetation to persist but are sufficiently mild to allow some species characteristic of warmer areas to grow and reproduce naturally. The average date of the earliest frost is December 3, with the latest being March 2, allowing an average growing season of 276 days. Intense summer showers account for much of the county's annual precipitation, which averages about 52 inches. The wettest months are June, July, and August with the driest being October and November. One of the driest years on record was 1954 when only 32.9 inches of rainfall was recorded on Sapelo Island. The wettest was seventy-five inches in 1964, a hurricane year. Several hurricanes from 1989-2005 passed near the Georgia coast but none caused serious damage. Most east coast hurricanes tend to follow the warmer waters of the offshore Gulf Stream. Brunswick, Georgia, just south of McIntosh County, is the westernmost point from the Gulf Stream of any section of the south Atlantic coast. Several historic hurricanes, however, have created extreme conditions that precipitated temporary economic chaos. The storms directly impacting McIntosh County with either landfall or severe effects, occurred in 1804, 1824, 1854, 1893, 1896, 1898, 1944, 1964 (Dora), 1979 (David), 2016 (Matthew) and 2017 (Irma). The worst of these were the 1824 and 1898 cyclones that left much of Sapelo and the nearby islands under several feet of water due to high tidal surge, as did Dora in 1964 and Irma in 2017. From 2016 through 2023, coastal Georgia has had impacting brushes with hurricanes or tropical storms each year.

INDEXES

Author's Family Referenced in Text

Index of People Other Than Author's Family

Places and Topics Mentioned in Text

178